RAILWAYS THROUGH AIREDALE & WHARFEDALE

C000182243

Martin Bairstow

"Jubilee" class 4 - 6 - 0 No 45692 "Cyclops" passing Newlay & Horsforth with the 7.58am (Saturdays Only) Derby to Glasgow St Enoch on 16 July 1960. *(David Holmes)*

Published by Martin Bairstow, 53 Kirklees Drive, Farsley, Leeds
Printed by The Amadeus Press, Cleckheaton, West Yorkshire

Contents

Acknowledgements

Thanks are due to everybody who has helped with the book. The articles and photographs are credited individually. The tickets and handbills are from the same people, plus David Beeken. The signal diagrams are from Richard Pulleyn, the maps my own. I have drawn information from **North of Leeds** and **Railways of Wharfedale** by Peter E Baughan. 'The Crumbling Edge of Quality' (page 44) is a quote from the late BR Chairman, Sir Peter Parker.

```
2576    2nd-    CHEAP   CHEAP    -2nd    2576
                SINGLE  SINGLE

                Skipton to

        Skipton                      Skipton
        Addingham                    Addingham

                ADDINGHAM

        (M)    1/4    Fare   1/4   (M)
        For conditions see over  For conditions see over
```

"Jubilee" No 45647 "Sturdee" coming off the goods line at Thwaites Junction with a Leeds to Carnforth freight on 15 April 1967.

(G W Morrison)

Travelling under the Axe

The lines featured in this book are those upon which I first became acquainted with the art of rail travel. My local station was Apperley Bridge and from the Spring of 1963 I was old enough to make journeys on my own. From September 1963, when I started at Bradford Grammar School, until March 1965, when both stations closed, I commuted between Apperley Bridge and Frizinghall. Throughout this period one journeyed under constant threat that the axe would soon fall.

In order to service about 75 passengers each weekday, Apperley Bridge boasted a station master, two clerks, two leading porters, a junior porter to clean the signal box windows etc, a vanman who distributed one van load of parcels each day around Rawdon and Yeadon and a goods checker who ensured that the odd wagon of coal in the goods yard had the right labels on.

My house was about one mile from the station and each morning I set off at the last minute and sprinted to catch the 8.25 train. One day I tripped and fell and needed the attention of the station first aid box. I don't suppose

that facility is available nowadays at stations manned only by a saver strip machine.

There were generally a few passengers about as I purchased my half return to Frizinghall for 7d but the main activity on the station was the listing on sheets of paper of the parcels which had arrived by train and were to be delivered by the van driver. The final column on these sheets was headed 'received in good order by' and the van driver used to invent the signatures of the recipients as he deposited each successive package in the doorway or coal house. Most of the parcels were mail order goods and most of the customers were out at work though it made little difference if they were in.

The train was a twin car Derby built dmu with only one car powered which was adequate for this route. Only on Summer Saturdays was it loaded up to eight cars because it then worked a Bradford Forster Square to Scarborough service. In all the 18 months, a train was never cancelled and I was late for school only once. There were plenty of minor delays, however, usually caused by

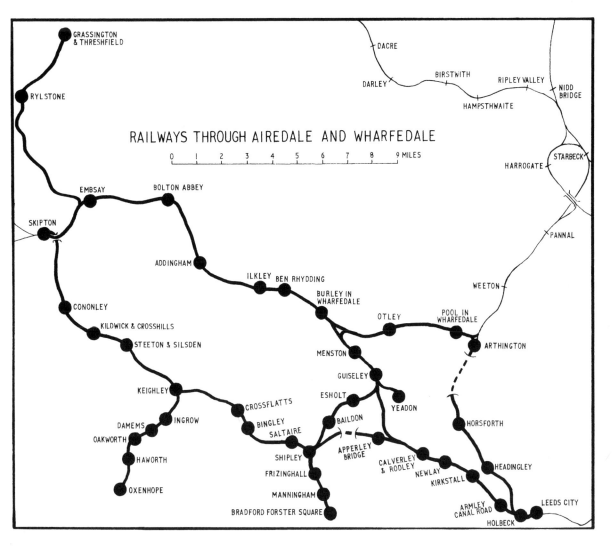

RAILWAYS THROUGH AIREDALE AND WHARFEDALE

time spent unloading parcels at Apperley Bridge and Shipley.

The quadruple track route was busy with both passenger and freight. My train was the 8.05 from Leeds which travelled on the 'fast' line and was overtaken just before reaching Apperley Bridge by the 8.10 dmu to Skipton, first stop Bingley. At least twice, this train was stopped at Apperley Bridge by the signalman, on instructions from control, to pick up one or two passengers for Keighley who would otherwise have been delayed by as much as 25 minutes through the 7.40 Leeds – Bradford running too late to catch its Skipton connection at Shipley. That was service.

Our arrival at Frizinghall was a couple of minutes before the 8.30 Bradford Forster Square – Morecambe called in the other direction. This was often 'Britannia' hauled but sometimes a 'Peak' class diesel. One morning I and a dozen other passengers used this train to get back from Manningham when our driver forgot to stop at Frizinghall. That is one of very few occasions that I have known trains miss booked stops. Frizinghall station had seen better days. The former buildings on the road bridge had been demolished and the booking office relocated in what had been a waiting room on the up platform. After September 1963, its last train was at 7.41 pm in order to save staffing costs although there were plenty of trains passing through after that hour. This type of false economy applied at quite a number of stations so that in the evening and on Sundays 'local' trains ran virtually non stop. This practice tended to die out later as one of the benefits of introducing unstaffed stations.

My grandparents moved to Ilkley in April 1964. Taking advantage of their new location in a rail served town, I lost little time in arranging a visit. From Apperley Bridge there were two ways of reaching Ilkley. The problem of going via Shipley was that, outside peak hours, the hourly interval trains gave about a ¾ hour wait in both directions. The alternative was to travel one station towards Leeds and change there. This possibility was usually thwarted by Ilkley trains not stopping at Calverley & Rodley but a Saturday afternoon visit was possible by this route.

In those days 'ordinary' single and return tickets could be purchased to any station on BR at 3d per mile provided that three days notice was given in the event of no fare for that destination having been calculated since the previous fares increase. But for selected local journeys 'cheap single' and 'day return' tickets were available often at less than half the 'ordinary' fare. I was sufficiently conversant with the arrangements to know that I would have to book separate day returns for the two sections of my journey.

One of the clerks was on duty in the booking office as I entered the station from the road bridge. The first preliminary towards obtaining a ticket was to knock on the booking office window in order that the person within might drop what he was doing, raise the hatch and begin to sell rail travel.

A half return to Calverley & Rodley please
What do you want to go there for?
I need to change there for Ilkley
Why don't you go via Shipley?
Because there isn't a connection
Well you'll have to book single both ways
But I want a return
It won't cost you any more

4F No 44586 with the pick up goods, resumes its journey towards the Sewage Works sidings at Apperley Viaduct, after shunting the yard at Apperley Bridge on 7 August 1963.   *(David Holmes)*

40114 in platform 1 at Ilkley, ready to leave with the 3.55pm to Leeds via Otley on 25 October 1958.
(David Holmes)

But I may not be able to get a ticket at Calverley &
Rodley on the way back (and if there's one thing to
which I object it is handing over excess fares at the
end of a journey without any receipt being issued.
In those days tickets were never sold on the train)
If I sell you a return I will have to cut a ticket in half
I'm sorry but I want a return ticket.

I stood my ground and duly exchanged 4d for an
Edmondson card ticket cut diagonally in half. The clerk's
grievance was that a printed child ticket was in issue for
single but not return journeys to Calverley & Rodley.

It only remained to descend the 42 steps to reach the
platform and join a two car dmu for the four minute
journey which compared very favourably with the time
required to buy the ticket.

Nobody joined the train at Calverley & Rodley and I
was the only one to alight. I stepped onto the platform
adjacent to where the station staff was standing. He
enquired: 'Is this where you want to be? Carvley?' (the
first I is not pronounced). I assured him that it was,
whereupon he invited the guard to proceed to the next
parish. He then followed me up the staircase towards the
ticket office.

A half return to Ilkley please

Without question an Edmondson card ticket (a
complete one this time) was put through the date stamp
in exchange for 1s6d, a sum I cheerfully disbursed
doubtless in anticipation of a grandparental grant. It was
only on the staircase back to the platform that I noticed
that the ticket bore the previous day's date. So once
again I disturbed the man's peace by knocking on the
booking office window to point out this defect in my

travel document. He said he didn't think anyone would
notice but he would alter the machine in case there were
any more customers. I took the opportunity of confirm-
ing that my train would be on platform 3, the down slow
line, since Ilkley trains could use either of the pairs of
tracks between Leeds and Apperley Junction.

The journey to Ilkley was accomplished in one of the
300 hp Derby built units which were introduced on this
line in 1959 and are still in operation. In those days they
were painted in lined green but the chevrons at each end
had given way to yellow warning panels. The front compartment in the trailer was reserved for first class
passengers but ordinary mortals could enjoy a front end
view when the power car was leading.

In 1964, the view beyond the immediate lineside was
much as it is today but the narrower view through the
front cab of that dmu was of a scene virtually unchanged
from Midland Railway days. At least all the facilities were
there even though some were a little decayed or falling
into disuse. Stored in sidings at Apperley Junction and
Calverley & Rodley, were sets of excursion coaches.
These were a familiar sight at a number of locations
before somebody decided that it was 'uneconomic' to
keep rolling stock for occasional use only.

The track was quadruple between Leeds and Shipley
whilst the Ilkley line was double throughout including the
extension to Skipton and the route through Otley which
still made its junctions at Menston and Burley. The
Yeadon branch still trailed in at Rawdon Junction. Every
station and junction had a signal box with a forest of
semaphore signals.

The stations nearly all had gas lighting of the 'modern'
type which had pilot lights. As a sign of neglect, only

those nearest the buildings were serviceable at most stations. It has become too much trouble to replace mantles at the extreme ends of the platforms. On the lines covered by this book, only Bradford Forster Square had fluorescent lights. Keighley and Armley Canal Road managed electric light bulbs but Arthington, Bolton Abbey and Embsay were still illuminated by oil lamps.

At each intermediate station, the arrival of the dmu was attended by a porter. Those with strong vocal chords shouted the name of the station. Other duties included closing the doors and collecting the tickets which at the end of the week had to be sorted into numerical order for every type and originating station and sent to an office in Newcastle. At Guiseley and Ilkley a platform barrow would be on hand for any parcels which might arrive on the train for delivery by road vehicle on Monday morning. Each goods yard still contained the odd wagon of coal.

On the return journey we hit Calverley & Rodley at the rush hour when within the space of two minutes there were three trains booked to call and on this day all three were there at once. As I alighted from the Ilkley – Leeds on platform 2, a Leeds – Skipton via Ilkley service was drawing into platform 3 (the other side of the centre island) but my sights were directed at the Leeds – Bradford local which was already standing at platform 1. The same leading porter was in attendance. On learning that I desired the Bradford train and pausing only to catch the attention of the driver of the Ilkley – Leeds, he escorted me across the track in front of it but to no avail. He assured me that there would be another one soon and proceeded up the staircase to his office.

A few minutes later he returned:

Did you just get off that train over there?
Yes
Where have you come from?
Ilkley
Where are you going?
Apperley Bridge
But what are you doing here?
Changing trains
And did you come here this dinner time?
Yes
Where were you going then?
From Apperley Bridge to Ilkley
And where are you going now?
From Ilkley to Apperley Bridge
Why didn't you go via Shipley?
Because there wasn't a connection.

He reaffirmed that I wouldn't have to wait long and went about his business again.

I recall once sitting on my bicycle outside Calverley & Rodley station when I observed the incumbent emerge from his booking office and throw his tealeaves out into the street. This was an unpleasant habit but how it summed up the gulf between the two worlds on either side of that station entrance. Just as that railman didn't care where the contents of his teapot landed once they had left railway property, so the public outside neither knew nor cared what travel facilities were available within that sanctum. With more than 50 departures each weekday, one could connect with services to any part of the BR system or beyond. But if you had tried to do so they would not have known what you were talking about.

The days when residents of Calverley would walk a mile and a half to start their journeys were long since past. The only way to have developed Calverley & Rodley

An oil lamp at Arthington, about to be extinguished for the last time on 20 March 1965.   *(John Holroyd)*

station would have been as a park and ride facility involving complete rebuilding. Failing this there was a strong case for eliminating such a remote station in order to accelerate journeys between centres of population. When the axe fell in 1965 it was a blunt instrument which landed indiscriminately on services both with and without potential.

Had it survived, Apperley Bridge station would have benefited from the greater freedom and affluence of what would have now been the railcard holding students at Woodhouse Grove School. It could also have offered car parking for commuters from Rawdon and Yeadon. Nowadays almost all local stations have car parks but in the 1960s the BR attitude was that such facilities 'encouraged people to use cars!'

Another station to shut its doors on 20 March 1965 was Saltaire. The official story now is that the replacement wooden halt opened in 1984 is both an architectural and a commercial success. Manned only by a saver strip machine but with platforms the right height, proper illumination and a better train service, it is claimed to be doing worthwhile business. There were one or two of us who objected to its closure in the first place.

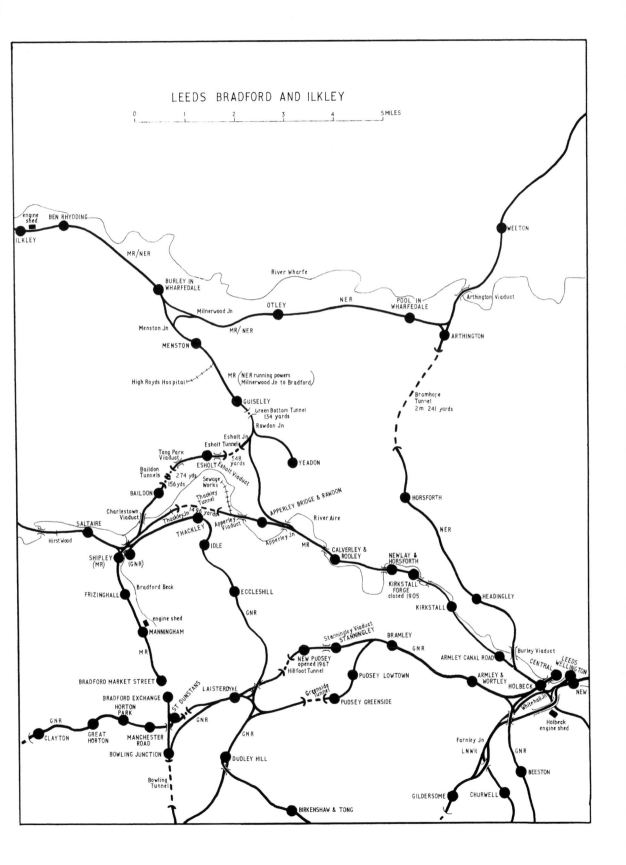

LEEDS BRADFORD AND ILKLEY

0   1   2   3   4   5 MILES

A Journey Through Airedale

42139 ready to leave Leeds City with the 1.36pm express to Bradford Forster Square, through from Bristol Temple Meads, on 1 February 1961. *(David Holmes)*

The present Leeds Station is an amalgam of the Midland Railway terminus at Wellington and the London & North Western and North Eastern Joint through station known as Leeds New. Wellington opened, with the Leeds & Bradford Railway, on 30 June 1846, bringing trains for the first time into the centre of Leeds. From the late 1840s the LNW and NE Companies shared the Midland facility at Wellington but traffic outgrew capacity so, on 1 April 1869, they opened their own adjacent Leeds New Station.

In 1938, Wellington and New were linked and renamed Leeds City but the LMS and LNER could not contemplate the works necessary to incorporate traffic still handled at the separate Leeds Central Station, 1/2 mile away. Finally, in 1959, BR embarked upon the project to concentrate all business at Leeds City. The scheme was halted, then begun again on a reduced basis, which assumed that many services would be closed under the Beeching Report.

What resulted in 1967, was a 12 platform passenger station, based on a slightly enlarged Leeds New, with Wellington reduced to a parcels facility. For the next 30 years, passengers were still able to use the entrance to Wellington, at the corner of City Square, but then had to negotiate a narrow fenced off part of the almost derelict, foul smelling Midland concourse to reach the inhabited part of the station.

Passenger facilities were poor. In particular, access to platforms 6 to 12 was via steps, a severe disincentive to elderly passengers and countless others encumbered with luggage, push chairs etc. In theory, you could ask the staff for assistance and someone would accompany you via the goods only lifts and overhead barrow way. I only tried this once, when Adrian was in a pram. The system didn't work. We missed a connection, which had a 16 minute margin. The station couldn't handle the volume of passengers, nor could it cope with the number of trains.

It had been designed at the height of the Beeching period when most local trains were expected to disappear and when half hourly, or even greater frequencies were undreamt of.

Eventually, in the late 1990s, work began on a scheme both to increase capacity and to improve passenger facilities. Completed in 2002, the remodelled station has 17 platforms, six through, nine west facing bays and two facing York. Communication between them is by escalators and passenger operated lifts. The Midland concourse has come back to life with new retail units. Some of

45589 "Gwalior" passing Holbeck with the southbound "Waverley" in 1959. A DMU out of Leeds Central is passing through the High Level station. *(Peter Sunderland)*

4F 0 - 6 - 0 No 43987 entering Holbeck Low Level with 2.55pm local from Leeds City to Bradford Forster Square on 28 June 1958. *(David Holmes)*

The road level booking hall at Armley Canal Road in September 1964. The building is still in existence.

(Geoffrey Lewthwaite)

At Calverley & Rodley, the stone building on platform 1 was in 1870s "Settle & Carlisle" style and must have been the focal point of the station prior to quadrupling at the turn of the Century when the overhead structure was built.

(Martin Bairstow collection)

Apperley Bridge was rebuilt for the widening to four tracks at the turn of the century. The large wooden building stood above the slow lines with a covered walkway bridging the fast lines.

(Dorothy Burrows collection)

the additional platforms are on land once occupied by the Midland Wellington Station.

There are now three pairs of tracks, curving away from Leeds Station. Crossovers allow flexibility but, in general, there is one pair for LNW traffic towards Huddersfield, one for GN trains to Doncaster and Bradford Interchange and the northernmost pair shared by the North Eastern route to Harrogate and Midland to Ilkley, Skipton and Bradford Forster Square.

The LNW and GN lines diverge at Whitehall Junction, just before the site of the two level Holbeck Station, closed in 1958. You can still see the cut away parapets, which carried the high level route out of Leeds Central.

Quadruple track continues to Wortley Junction, where the Harrogate line curves off to the right, leaving Midland traffic to cross onto the left hand pair of tracks, which continue as what used to be the slow lines towards Shipley. For the short distance to Armley Canal Road, the fast line formation, on the right, has been built over. For most of the rest of the way to Shipley, the fast line formation is clear and used as a track for maintenance vehicles to drive along.

When the route was quadrupled, in stages around 1900, the original line was slewed in places. Sometimes the additional lines were laid on the north side, elsewhere to the south. When the line

was reduced to double in 1967, they simply removed the fast lines. "Fast" meant direct from Leeds to Bradford. It did not refer to the speed of the traffic. Frequently, you could see a Leeds - Bradford stopper, on the fast being overtaken by an Anglo Scots express on the slow. The fast lines were on the north side from Leeds as far as the flyover, which carried them over the slow lines between Armley and Kirkstall.

The 11 miles from Leeds to Shipley is covered non-stop in as many minutes. The intermediate stations were closed in 1965. All had been rebuilt around 1900 with four platforms and their main buildings up above at road level. All have vanished completely, apart from the booking hall at Armley Canal Road, which has been restored by the tenant. Each of the stations had an attendant goods yard. The goods sheds can still be seen, in alternative use, at Kirkstall and Calverley & Rodley. At Apperley Bridge the goods yard was in the angle formed by the diverging Ilkley line, where new houses have been built. In addition to the public goods facilities, there were private rail systems at Kirkstall Power Station, Kirkstall Forge and Esholt Sewerage Works. There were so many signal boxes that, in many instances, the outer and inner distants for one box were mounted beneath the home and starter of the previous one, giving a forest of semaphores the whole way. The only colour light signals were the

8F 2 - 8 - 0 passing Calverley & Rodley on the "up slow" line with a train of empty mineral wagons on 16 April 1961. A rake of spare carriages awaits the Summer holiday period.   (G W Morrison)

To one who remembers the "old" railway, the stretch between Leeds and Shipley is just a desert, two plain tracks and not a lot else. Two class 31s pass the site of Kirkstall Station with a loaded Tilcon train from the Grassington branch, spreading a cloud of limestone dust. At that time, this was virtually the only freight traffic through Airedale, the Settle & Carlisle route having been closed to goods for political reasons. There has since been a significant revival.
(Martin Bairstow)

Bradford Forster Square regained a handful of London trains in October 1988. 43195 brings up the rear of a High Speed Train, passing the site of Newlay & Horsforth in 1989.
(Martin Bairstow)

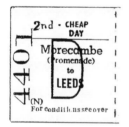

A class 144 passing the site of Calverley & Rodley with a Leeds - Ilkley service in February 1991. This was the week when a BR apologist famously blamed delays on the "wrong kind of snow".
(Martin Bairstow)

0 - 4 - 0ST "Elizabeth" is passing through Apperley Bridge on 27 October 1958, en route from its makers at Hudswell Clarke, Leeds to the private system at Esholt Sewage Works. *(J C W Halliday)*

Apperley Junction up fast and slow starters, which incorporated the Calverley & Rodley distants. The levers had short handles to remind the signalman not to use his full strength when "pulling off"

The ten arch Apperley Viaduct, still in use, is the one built for the widening in 1900. The disused structure alongside was built in 1867, following collapse of the original. The viaduct is one of eight crossings of the River Aire, between Leeds and Shipley. The Railway also crosses the Leeds & Liverpool Canal four times. One of the canal bridges occurs between Apperley Viaduct and Thackley Tunnel. The private branch to Esholt Sewerage Works used to run along the canal side from this point. Thackley Tunnel comprises two double track bores. The one in use dates from 1900. Luckily, it had enough clearance to take 25kv electric wires. The original, from 1846, has been disused since closure of the fast lines in 1967.

Shipley is the hub of the network with all except Leeds - Ilkley traffic passing through. The weekday off peak timetable gives 16 electric departures an hour, to which can be added the longer distance diesel trains.

Prior to 1979, the station had platforms only on the lines leading to Bradford. Historically, this arrangement worked fairly well as the service was based mainly on trains running from Leeds to Bradford and from Bradford to Skipton, Leeds -

Skipton passengers often having to change at Shipley.

When most local trains were withdrawn in March 1965, Shipley became dependent on Leeds to Skipton DMUs. In the Leeds bound direction, these used to stop first in platform 2, then go forward to beyond Bradford Junction, cross over and come back into platform 3. There, the tail lamp was removed from the front end, by a member of the station staff, whilst a spare one was picked up by the guard and placed on the rear buffer beam.

At first, Skipton bound trains followed the same procedure but they soon decided that it was easier to continue beyond Bingley Junction and set back into platform 1. The driver remained in the front (Skipton end) cab, putting the engines into reverse, whilst the guard rode in cab at the other end for the duration of the manoevre. An early morning passenger / parcels train was advertised as starting from Shipley, though in fact it came from Leeds, because it had a van in the rear. This meant there was no rear cab in which the guard could sit reversing into Shipley so, under the rules, it could not be a passenger train.

A single main line platform (No 5) was provided for Leeds - Skipton trains in May 1979. A year later, signalling alterations were made to allow stopping trains in the other direction to cross over and pass "wrong line" through platform 5. That was the

42072 entering Shipley platform 3 with a Bradford to Leeds train on 5 May 1963.
(John Oxley)

The Booking Hall at Shipley in March 1973, still gas lit and heated by a stove. There was an atmosphere of neglect. For as long as I could remember, the window facing onto platform 3 had been lettered "..oak Room and .arcel Office". The place was refurbished in 1999 and is now a great deal more inviting.
(Stuart Baker)

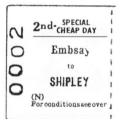

By 1987, platforms 3 an 4 had been shortened and opened up to the elements. The 3 foot dial Potts clock had not worked for years. It had two faces on each of platforms 2 and 3, connected by rodding from within the booking office. *(F W Smith)*

Bringing imported coal, landed in Scotland, 66093 waits for a signal in platform 1 at Shipley on 1 August 2001.   *(Martin Bairstow)*

arrangement until 1992 when, as part of the electrification work, a platform was built for the Leeds bound track. This took the number 1, left vacant when the Bradford to Skipton curve was reduced to single track as part of the 1980 alterations. Platforms 2 and 5 then exchanged identities so that 1 and 2 serve the main line, 3 and 4 the Bradford to Leeds and Ilkley lines and 5 Bradford to Skipton.

A "casualty" of electrification was the remaining traditional block signalling. For some reason, the boxes at the three corners of Shipley triangle had been Shipley Bradford Junction and Shipley Bingley Junction but just Leeds Junction. Post 1994, they are marked with small signs proclaiming, respectively, Shipley South, West and East Junctions. Nearby, the former Guiseley Junction is now Dockfield Junction.

Saltaire is the model village, built by Titus Salt in the 1850s, when he moved his manufacturing plant out of Bradford. The village is laid out on a grid. Such is the problem of traffic congestion, that tourists are now urged to arrive by public transport. Dr Beeching's contribution was to close the station in 1965. It reopened on the same site in 1984. Some visitors head for Shipley Glen, half a mile away, across the River and beyond the Victoria Park. Having walked that far, you can take the last 400 yards on the Shipley Glen Tramway, a double track cable line of 1ft 8in gauge, opened in 1895, which ascends at an average of 1 in 8.

The route from Shipley to Skipton was never quadrupled throughout but, from Bingley to Thwaites, there were goods roads on the outside of the two passenger lines. Midway along this section was Marley Junction which, despite its name, was not a convergence of routes but just a cross over between goods and passenger lines.

Crossflatts is a wooden halt opened in 1982. The Midland Railway always held out against a station here. They did, however yield to pressure for passenger facilities at Thwaites but found the response disappointing. There is no visible evidence of the station, which closed in 1909, after a life of only 17 years.

Keighley is the one of the few stations, where you can see steam, diesel and electric trains in regular service. With luck, you may see one of each simultaneously in the three normal departure platforms. The station is built on the junction with the Worth Valley branch. It has two long platforms (1 and 2) on the main line and two shorter ones (3 and 4) curving away on the branch. There was also an unnumbered bay platform at the Leeds end of platform 1. This was filled in about 1965. The platforms are all bare, except for a length of original canopy on No 4. The Keighley & Worth Valley Railway does have some spare, matching bits of canopy, acquired from Rotherham Masborough, but these have not yet been re-used.

The station was opened in its present position on 6 May 1883. It fronts onto Bradford Road, which crosses the Railway on a bridge. This was built in 1880 to replace the previous level crossing. The expanded passenger facility was partly in anticipation of the Great Northern Railway arriving

Saltaire Station was built in 1856 to serve Titus Salt`s model village. The low platforms remained until closure in 1965. The steps down onto the Shipley bound platform were the only part of the original station incorporated into the 1984 reopening. They have since been replaced by a ramp.
(Martin Bairstow collection)

The last day of the old Bingley Station, which stood in front of the Three Rise Lock. It was replaced by the present structure on 24 July 1892.
(Peter E Baughan collection)

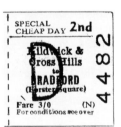

A Skipton to Bradford DMU restarts from Bingley on 22 June 1964. *(Peter E Baughan)*

18 months later, also to free the site of the old station for expansion of the goods yard.

At one time, the Midland goods yard was shunted 24 hours a day. It closed completely in 1981 and the site is now occupied by Sainsburys. Between 1884 and 1961, there was also a Great Northern goods depot, just across the road from the Midland but nearly two miles by transfer freight via G N Junction. How things have reversed. The growth of road transport and the decline of heavy industry have combined to kill all the freight. Yet the passenger station is busier than ever before.

Between Keighley and Skipton, the Aire Valley is wide, the land undulating and the gradient easy. Steeton & Silsden is the third station, more or less on the same sight. The present facility was built in 1990 when the station reopened after an absence of 25 years. The road bridge replaced the level crossing about the same time. Part of the original 1847 station stands opposite the present up platform. The 1888 structure was on the Skipton side of the level crossing. The station does good business. The car park is often full. Patronage may be inflated by the fares system, which encourages car borne commuters to drive to this, the last station in the PTE area, rather than Cononley or Skipton.

Kildwick & Crosshills was originally on the Skipton side of the level crossing. This is still the busiest level crossing in Airedale, though it no longer accommodates the main road, thanks to the bypass, which now runs from east of Bingley to beyond Skipton. There have been threats to extend the Trunk Road further towards Leeds, involving demolition of Saltaire Village but this seems to have abated.

Kildwick Station was resited in 1889, ¼ mile nearer to Skipton. It closed in 1965. There have been proposals for reopening, so far without result. At Cononley, the platforms were never removed during 23 years of closure, so reopening in 1988 was relatively cheap.

For the last mile and a half into Skipton from Snaygill, there were again four tracks, reduced back to two in 1967. The former Ilkley line, now the quarry branch to Rylstone, crosses over on a viaduct as the main line curves to the left, past the site of the original Skipton Station, more recently the goods yard and now a Morrisons supermarket.

Skipton Station opened on its present site on 1 May 1876, the day the Settle & Carlisle line opened for passengers. There were four platforms in the main station, to which two were added at a slightly higher level on the south side when the Ilkley line opened in 1888. The station declined in importance with closure of the lines to Ilkley in 1965 and Colne in 1970. Only two platforms remained in use until electrification brought the whole of the main station back into use.

The electric wires continue a little way beyond the station to the depot, situated on the north side of the line, opposite the steam shed, which closed in 1967.

8F 2 - 8 - 0 No 48533 with a train of empty mineral wagons passing Keighley in June 1953. The goods yard on the right is now Sainsburys. *(J Davenport)*

In 1875, the Midland Railway declined a request for a station at Crossflatts, claiming that it was too close to Bingley. The question reappeared from time to time but it was not until 1982 that anything was done.

A Leeds - Skipton three car Metro Cammell set calls there on 22 May 1982, during the first week of operation. At first, traffic was disappointing. Perhaps the Midland had been right. But since the PTE built a car park in the mid 1990, business has picked up.

(Martin Bairstow)

The Keighley Gas Works diesel, shunting the private sidings alongside the main line at Thwaites Junction in early 1956.

(Peter Sunderland)

Kildwick & Crosshills, looking towards Skipton, shortly before closure in 1965.

(Geoffrey Lewthwaite)

Cononley reopened in 1988 but without the buildings.

(Geoffrey Lewthwaite)

8F 2 - 8 - 0 No 48652 passing Utley, between Steeton and Keighley, on 14 April 1962 with what appears to be the Heysham to Billingham ammonia train diverted this way for some reason.

(Martin Bairstow collection)

"Peak" class No D25 with the 10.25 Leeds City to Glasgow St Enoch at Skipton on 7 July 1965. The Ilkley line platforms 5 and 6 are on the extreme right.

(M Mitchell)

And Through Wharfedale

The six platform terminus at Bradford Market Street, opened in 1897 and renamed Forster Square in 1924. The two locomotives are 0 - 4 - 4Ts. Posters advertise Belfast, Ingleton, Morecambe, Connemara and the Norwegian Fjords.   *(Martin Bairstow collection)*

One of the failings of the early railway builders was their leaving cities such as Bradford with two dead end stations when one central installation would have been just as easy to accomplish in the days before the city centre properties were built.

Not that the two Bradford Stations were far apart. I can remember when each displayed tangerine enamel signs offering directions to the other, "five minutes via Petergate". Since then, they have got farther apart. First Exchange Station retreated ¼ mile out in 1973. Then Forster Square moved a similar distance the other way in 1990. Now the gap is three times what it used to be.

You can still enter the old Forster Square site but all you find is a footpath leading into or past the Tax office. They used to call the Tax offices Bradford 1, Bradford 2 and so on but now they are Bradford Midland, Valley View and Beckside. I've yet to have the pleasure of visiting these new offices, though I'm sure the routine is the same. The client under investigation will have told me repeatedly that he's "got nothing to hide". He will tell the Inspector that he hasn't been able to afford a holiday for seven years nor a new suit for at least five. Then he comes out with some revelation, which is always prefaced by "I don't know if I ought to be telling you

this....but". I cringe as the client proceeds to hang himself. Don't mock it, these Inland Revenue staff can amount to a lot of commuter traffic and the station could hardly be more convenient.

Inside the Booking Hall, now called Travel Centre, a small plaque records that from this Station, the first British Pullman train departed on I August 1874. Actually, this must refer to a predecessor station but one under a previous name but one.

There are three platforms in the 1990 structure. The island, Nos 1 and 2, is so long that Stuart Baker once suggested putting an exit at the far end and calling it Manningham. Two or three times a day, this platform fulfils its intended purpose by accommodating a GNER class 91 on a London train. Otherwise, activity revolves around the three half hourly services to Leeds, Ilkley and Skipton.

To the east of the present station are acres of level ground, a rare feature in Bradford, which used to be railway land. It was not until Manningham Junction that the formation narrowed down to just four tracks, two passenger and two goods. The present route swings over to the goods lines at the site of Manningham Junction so as to bypass Manningham Station, after which it slews back onto the old passenger side. To the east of Manningham

LNER 4 - 4 - 0 No 2027 calls at Manningham on 2 March 1946 with a Harrogate to Bradford Forster Square train. The decline of this service is featured in *Railways Around Harrogate Volume Three*.
(G H Butland)

Standard class 5 No 73053 passing Frizinghall with an express for Bradford Forster Square in September 1955.
(D Thompson/ F W Smith collection)

A choice of route, approaching Shipley Bradford Junction. The passenger lines, on the left have two options, the goods lines three. In each case, the distant signal for the next box is mounted below the junction signal.

In 1904, the goods lines were extended from Bradford Junction to Leeds Junction passing behind platform 4. This enabled Leeds to Bradford freight movements to avoid conflict with Skipton to Bradford passenger traffic but the facility was removed in 1969.
(M A King/ F W Smith collection)

Station is another expanse of level ground, long redeveloped, which used to house the engine shed and carriage sidings.

Frizinghall is an unstaffed halt with staggered platforms. There used to be an extensive goods yard on the right hand side with private sidings into a large mill. Approaching Shipley, on the left the goods depot is still in use as a scrap yard with internal shunters, including "Prince of Wales", which started life on the Esholt Sewerage Works system.

Shipley Station is a triangle, though not a perfect one like Queensbury, where the platforms met at all three corners. The Ilkley train takes platform three, which was shortened in the days of rationalisation, but then extended beyond its original length to accommodate complete London trains. It is signalled both ways for the benefit of long "Inter City" trains but incoming locals pass through platform four, which is reached via the subway. Platform three is on a right hand curve. In steam days, the guard of a long train might venture a long way from his van before the driver could see his green flag or lamp. There was an occasion in 1964, and may well have been others, when he was too slow to get back on board. The goods lines from Bradford passed behind platform four, feeding in to the passenger lines just before Leeds Junction box. Here the main line curved alongside giving quadruple track all the way to Leeds. The Ilkley train had to cross right over to take the branch at Guiseley Junction. Now the main line is only double track and the branch reduced to single.

Seeing the heavy engineering on the Shipley to Guiseley, it is easy to appreciate why they delayed building this for 11 years after the rest of the Otley & Ilkley system. A bridge over the canal is followed by Charlestown Viaduct, which spans both the River Aire and the main road. Approaching Baildon, there is a housing estate on the site of the goods yard. The main station building is in Settle & Carlisle style, thanks to the 1876 opening date. It went out of railway use during the 20 year period that Baildon Station was closed.

The track was singled in 1983. Ten years later, it was slewed onto the middle of the formation to assist electrification through Baildon Nos 1 and 2 Tunnels. Tong Park Viaduct is a stone structure of ten arches. A short tunnel leads under the Bradford to Ilkley road and into the site of Esholt Station, closed in 1940 and demolished about 12 years later. Access to the goods yard, closed in 1953, was by a ground frame on the platform. The late Geoff Butland recalled an incident in the 1920s. The station master had set the signals at danger following departure of an all stations Ilkley to Bradford train and thought he had sufficient time to pay a call before the Harrogate to Bradford was due. He was disturbed by the whistle of the LNER train, which was not booked to stop at Esholt. He emerged with his trousers at half mast, made a dash for the ground frame and "pulled off".

When the station closed on Saturday 26 October 1940, Geoff Butland was so disgusted that he travelled on the last train without paying his fare. The following Monday, an aggrieved commuter had a *Telegraph & Argus* reporter travel with him to record his pulling the communication cord as the train passed through Esholt. It came to a stand some distance beyond the station.

DMUs used to pass noisily through the 548 yard Esholt Tunnel but the class 333 electrics are pretty soundproof. At Esholt Junction, the route joins the double track from Leeds, which has climbed at 1 in 60 since leaving the Aire Valley at Apperley Junction.

Up until the late 1970s, there was a severe speed restriction for trains taking the Ilkley line at Apperley Junction. As a result, trains could make a heavy job of the climb. I can just remember, the spectacle and sound of steam hauled freight attacking the incline. I have certainly experienced 300 hp DMUs (power car and trailer) struggling in low gear. Nowadays, you just notice a slight lurch as the electric takes the 50 mph cross over at Apperley Junction. The gradient makes no impression whatever as the train negotiates two short tunnels, Hindles and Apperley Lane, before passing through woodlands overlooking Esholt Sewerage Works.

When the track was singled in 1983, the section ran almost to Guiseley Station, the last stretch in parallel to the track from Bradford. In 1994, capacity was increased by recommencing double track at the entrance to Springs Tunnel, 1/4 mile before Esholt Junction, which became an effective junction again.

1/4 mile beyond Esholt Junction, an electrical substation marks the site of Rawdon Junction, where the short Yeadon branch trailed in.

Still visible at Guiseley are the platform extensions, which used to permit carriages to be set back when trains from Bradford and Leeds were remarshalled for Otley and Ilkley. The footbridge was replaced during electrification work. The old Midland one has found a new life at Kirkby Stephen. Guiseley became an unstaffed halt in October 1968. The buildings were subsequently demolished but a new ticket office and waiting rooms were commissioned in 2002. Inside are some framed photographs of the previous structures.

High Royds Hospital stands about 1/2 mile to the west of the Railway, between Guiseley and Menston. Between 1883 and 1951, coal deliveries were made via a private siding. Access from the main line was by a ground frame. The Hospital had its own shunting engine, steam at first, but in 1897 the line was electrified.

The short, 38 yard Otley & Bradford Road Tunnel brings the line into Menston Station, where the goods yard had coal deliveries until June 1982. The site is now a car park for commuters. This might not have been possible, had the yard closed in the Beeching rather than PTE era and the land been sold. The station buildings somehow survived the long period as an unstaffed halt. They were refurbished in 1998 when booking facilities returned.

Half a mile further, at Menston Junction, the signal box was on the left, opposite the point where

The 11.33 Ilkley to Bradford leaving Baildon on 10 November 1979. Since February 1983, the line has been single and this platform disused. The signal is a fixed distant for Guiseley Junction, Shipley. *(Martin Bairstow)*

Esholt Station, which closed in 1940, looking towards Bradford.
(Dorothy Burrows collection)

Milnerwood Junction in March 1965 with the Ilkley line veering right and the Bradford route attacking the gradient. The line closed on the first weekend of July 1965, but the box was used to work the points for the demolition trains the following year.
(F W Smith)

A WD 2 - 8 - 0 heads an eastbound freight through Otley in Summer 1961   *(Peter E Baughan)*

The Otley and Ilkley branch platforms at Arthington in Summer 1961.   *(Peter E Baughan)*

At Menston, both the main building and "up" side shelter survived 30 years as an unstaffed halt. They were brought back into use when staff were reintroduced in 1998. *(D Butterfield)*

At Burley in Wharfedale, the former Otley & Ilkley Joint building was not so lucky. Last used in 1968, it was demolished five years later. The station remains unstaffed.
(D Butterfield)

Ben Rhydding opened a year later than Burley. The distinctive building here was also demolished after the withdrawal of staff in 1968.
(D Butterfield)

the Otley line began its 1 in 59 descent. Curving sharply to the right, this soon came alongside the Otley & Ilkley Joint line where both crossed the Bradford to Ilkley main road on separate structures. A further mile was required for the two lines to achieve the same height and fuse at Milnerwood Junction.

The abandoned Menston Junction to Otley route is potentially retrievable as far as the outskirts of Otley, where the bypass has taken the track bed through Otley Station and beyond. The main building at Otley was in similar style to the one which can still be seen at Ilkley. It was situated on the Arthington bound platform. A subway led to the island platform, whose inner face was for trains to Ilkley and outer one a loop for Midland trains starting to Bradford.

Beyond Otley, the line continued in sole North Eastern ownership. To the north, the Wharfe Valley widens but on the south side, the land rises steeply towards Otley Chevin. Pool in Wharfedale had staggered platforms, that on the down (Ilkley) side being an island. The site is now a housing estate.

At Arthington, the Otley branch joined the Leeds - Harrogate line by a triangular junction. Before the branch opened in 1865, the station, then called Pool, was near Arthington North, where the Pool to Harewood road passes under. The 1865 station was at the Leeds apex of the triangle, with diverging platforms on the branch. The main buildings stood within the triangle, as did the detached house of the station master. This last item is still there, virtually the sole reminder that there ever was a station at Arthington.

Returning to the operational Wharfedale Line, this descends at 1 in 88 from Menston towards Burley in Wharfedale. I have known a first generation DMU struggle up this modest gradient during leaf fall season. With only one power car and a trailer, slipping and just about maintaining walking speed, the guard came round to ascertain that nobody wanted to alight at Menston, where luckily there was nobody waiting on the platform. The train kept up its slow progress without stopping until it safely reached the summit in Guiseley Station. This would be on an evening as, even in the 1970s, you wouldn't find many trains doing no business at Menston.

The Otley line trailed in at Burley Junction, a short distance before Burley in Wharfedale Station. Houses have been built on the site of the goods yard, hopefully increasing the number of commuters. For the remaining $3\frac{1}{4}$ miles to Ilkley, the line clings to the hillside. The "Cow and Calf" rocks can be seen on Ilkley Moor, overlooking Ben Rhydding.

The two platforms in use at Ilkley broadly represent the original Otley & Ilkley Joint station of 1865. They have turned the buffer stop end into a supermarket and have then had to extend the platforms at the outer end so that each can accommodate two four coach trains. As a result, the operational part of the station is almost all outside

Bank Holiday crowds on platform 4 at Ilkley, waiting for their return train to come through from Bolton Abbey, about 1961.
(Ilkley Gazette)

"Patriot" class 4 - 6 - 0 No 45505 "The Royal Army Ordnance Corps" leaving Ilkley with the 6.45pm return half day excursion from Whaley Bridge on 15 May 1955. *(F W Smith)*

"Crab" 2 - 6 -0 No 42857 crossing Brook Street Bridge, possibly with another return excursion into Lancashire, Summer 1955. *(Sybil Parry, F W Smith collection)*

The Skipton line left Ilkley by a 25 arch viaduct.
(John Robinson/ F W Smith collection)

and crossed Addingham Main Street by a wrought iron bridge. The station was to the left.
(John Robinson/ F W Smith collection)

2 - 6 - 2T No 40112 arriving at Addingham with a local from Bradford Forster Square to Skipton in May 1958.
(Peter Sunderland)

Addingham, looking towards Skipton in 1958.   *(Peter Sunderland)*

the range of the canopies. The main building is well preserved, mostly in retail but non - railway use. The ticket office, closed in 1968, was finally replaced in 1997. During 29 years as an unstaffed halt, a chargeman was still employed to attend the station but not to serve passengers. Until 1988, his duties included switching on the gas lights.

The Skipton line left the Otley & Ilkley Joint at the entrance to the station and passed through platforms 3 and 4 on a rising gradient. The island platform, Nos 2 and 3 was level at the outer end but gradually acquired a slant as it tried to reconcile the ascending Skipton line with the level terminal track. Steps were needed to board trains in platform 3, which remained in use until 1983.

A description of the next six route miles is, inevitably in the past tense. The railway passed through an opening in the end wall of Ilkley Station and, immediately crossed Brook Street on a girder bridge. It continued its elevated passage through the town with the 386 yard Ilkley Viaduct, comprising 25 spans of varying length. There followed an embankment, interspaced with stone bridges over a number of side roads, then two skew bridges over the A65 main road.

Addingham Station was a stone structure, with the main building on the Ilkley platform. At this point the Railway was supported by a 30 ft high retaining wall on the north side. This wall was pierced by the station entrance, which led into the subway, which

was also the means of communication between the two platforms. On leaving the station, the line crossed Addingham Main Street by a wrought iron bridge. About a mile further on, it passed over Lob Ghyll by a five arch viaduct, which still stands, hidden in trees.

At Bolton Abbey we can return to the present tense. Outwardly, the design of the new station is based on that of the old, but inside it is better appointed. There are no oil lamps nor chemi loos, but the Manager's office does display some antique furniture and fittings. The biggest addition compared with the old regime is the catering facility. One thing which hasn't changed is the proximity, or lack of it, to Bolton Abbey itself. In BR days, Bill Smith used to get alighting passengers asking where was the Abbey. Today, the Railway anticipates the question by issuing a leaflet setting out the walking routes and implying, I suspect falsely, that King George V actually legged it on his visits.

Not yet operational, is the former Guiseley signal box, positioned at the Embsay end of the station. The old box was at the Ilkley end. Bill Smith has the last train register from Bolton Abbey and will be happy for it to carry the first entries when the new box is commissioned.

The present track is single. Previously it was double, except when they lifted one line between Addingham and Embsay during the First World War. The second track was replaced in 1921.

To pass trains about half way between Bolton Abbey and Embsay, a new signal box has been built at Stoneacre, a place which did not feature in the previous history of the line. The brick signal box is based on Daisyfield, near Blackburn. Embsay box is well restored and functional on its original site. The station appears in 1888 condition, at least outwardly. Most of the main building is now a shop. The porters' room makes a small café. The ticket office function has been transferred to an outbuilding, which used to serve as a taxi hut at Ilkley Station.

The main source of traffic at Embsay used to be the quarry, which was accessed by a spur from the down sidings, just to the east of the station. The quarry had an internal rail system with two locomotives, "Wyvern" and "Darfield", two generations of each. The second "Darfield" was a 0-6-0ST, built by Hudswell Clarke in 1934 and scrapped in 1952, after which a road tractor was used to shunt wagons within the quarry.

Another outlet from the quarry was by a wagonway, a rather crude railway extending from the quarry to the Springs Branch of the Leeds & Liverpool Canal, near Skipton Castle. About 1895, the wagonway was converted into a standard gauge railway, worked by rope haulage, and connected, via the quarry system, to the spur from the Midland. The wagonway closed about 1950.

The preserved railway ends in a run round loop, a few yards before Embsay Junction, where the single track Rylstone branch trails in. There is no physical connection between the two railways. The branch continues as single line, over what was the double track formation, passing first through a tubular tunnel under the Skipton bypass, then the more conventional Hawbank Tunnel, 219 yards in length. A succession of bridges carry the line over the Leeds & Liverpool Canal, the main road and the Aire Valley railway. The descent continues through platform 5, at Skipton Station until the line reaches the level of the Aire Valley route at Skipton Station North Junction. Here there used to be a conventional junction, allowing traffic from Wharfedale to continue to Carlisle, Morecambe or Colne. Today the line ends in a siding and run round loop because quarry traffic from Rylstone all proceeds in Leeds direction.

For the opening of the Ilkley line, in 1888, platforms 5 and 6 were provided with buildings and full length canopies, but the latter were removed in LMS days. In my recollection, from about December 1963, the Ilkley line platforms were just an afterthought to the busy main line station. A man had gone round with a long pole switching on the gas lights in the main station but platform 5 was ignored until it was nearly time for the 5.08pm departure to Bradford via Ilkley. Even then, only a short length of platform was lit.

WD 2 - 8 - 0 No 90377 attacking the climb out of Skipton towards Ilkley with the Heysham Moss to Billingham ICI ammonia train in May 1959. *(Peter Sunderland)*

"Compound" 4 - 4 - 0 No 41063 heads a Skipton to Bradford via Ilkley train over the main line whilst 2 - 6 - 2T No 41284 takes a local via Keighley in April 1958. *(Peter Sunderland)*

"Compound" 4 - 4 - 0 No 41101 prepares to restart from Skipton with a Morecambe to Leeds semi fast on 18 June 1958. *(J C W Halliday)*

Construction and Development

The Leeds & Bradford Railway

The first eleven miles of railway through the Aire Valley as far as Shipley were conceived as a link between the cities of Leeds and Bradford. Leeds had enjoyed the benefit of railway communication since 1834 when the Leeds & Selby Railway had opened from a terminus at Marsh Lane in the east end of the city. The opening on 1 July 1840 of the North Midland Railway placed Leeds at the end of a continuous line from London and from the Midlands.

Bradford was already established as the centre of the wool textile industry but was nine miles from the nearest railway facilities either at Leeds or at 'Brighouse for Bradford' station in the Calder Valley.

There were two routes by which a railway might be built between Leeds and Bradford. The early 1830s had seen the unsuccessful promotion of a 'short line' which would have taken a direct course via Stanningley involving gradients of the order of 1 in 50. The alternative to the 'short line' was a 'valley line' following the route of the canal via Shipley. The distance would be 13 ½ miles but the gradients relatively easy. The 'valley line' was favoured by George Stephenson who had surveyed a route in 1838 whilst working on the North Midland project.

On 22 December 1843, a provisional committee was formed to manage the affairs of the Leeds & Bradford Railway Company pending its formal incorporation by Act of Parliament on 4 July 1844. The chairman was George Hudson, the 'Railway King'.

This gentleman, who lived from 1800 until 1871, became one of the richest men in York following the death of an uncle in 1827. Hudson used his wealth both to indulge himself and to bribe his way into local politics. He became Lord Mayor of York in 1838 and eventually entered Parliament as member for Sunderland in 1845. Meanwhile he had acquired an interest in railways becoming the first chairman of the York & North Midland Railway in 1836.

By the mid 1840s, a quarter of the country's railways were under Hudson's control. The largest component in Hudson's empire was the Midland Railway, formed in 1844 by the amalgamation of the North Midland, Midland Counties and Derby & Birmingham Junction Railways which together stretched from the Midlands to Leeds.

It would have been logical for the Leeds & Bradford Railway to have been viewed as an extension of the Midland especially with Hudson as its chairman and Stephenson as engineer. Amalgamation did follow in 1846 but the circumstances by which this was achieved proved to be a turning point in the career of Hudson leading to his 'dethronement' in 1848.

On 30 December 1843, the Provisional Committee of the Leeds & Bradford Railway met to allot shares. These had been oversubscribed and the numbers allotted to most applicants were scaled down but Hudson and his deputy chairman, John Waddingham, made sure that they got the numbers they wanted. The shares would then immediately acquire a premium value leaving it open to Hudson and his associate to make a very substantial capital gain.

Construction work began immediately on receiving

40074 at Leeds City with the 12.16 to Ilkley via Otley on 2 February 1955. *(David Holmes)*

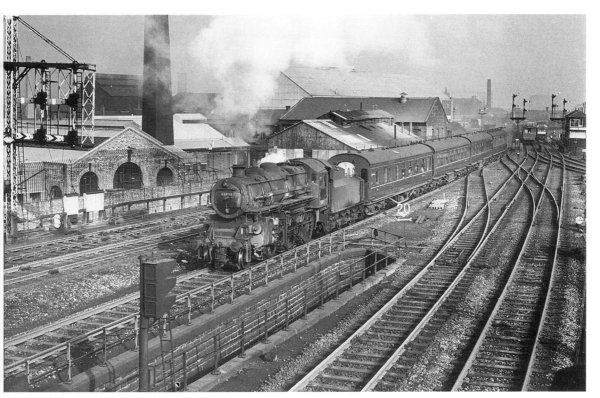

43039 approaching Holbeck with the 5.31pm from Leeds City to Ilkley via Otley on 19 April 1962. This train remained steam hauled until September 1962.   *(David Holmes)*

Parliamentary sanction in July 1844 and was completed in just under two years. The official opening on 30 June 1846 was marked by a public holiday in Bradford. The Leeds terminus at Wellington Station was also used by Midland Railway trains from 1 July 1846.

In common with many contemporary railways, the Leeds & Bradford was opened at the first opportunity. The company was anxious to get trains moving and income flowing almost as soon as the track was laid. The provision of intermediate stations had to come later. For about a fortnight all trains ran non stop then temporary arrangements were made for a station at Shipley. By the end of July, Apperley Bridge, Calverley Bridge (as it was then called) and Kirkstall had all appeared in the timetable. Newlay came later in 1846 and Armley the following year. Permanent structures were eventually provided at all these but not at the short lived Idle station. This appears to have lasted about 12 months between September 1847 and September 1848. It was the result of pressure from the village of Idle for a station at the west end of Thackley Tunnel. It was evidently not a success.

In order to win support for its 1844 Bill, the Leeds & Bradford Railway had committed itself to extensions from Shipley to Keighley and from Bradford to Halifax. As regards Keighley, the company quickly honoured its obligation.

Events concerning the Halifax proposal were rather more complicated. A nominally independent West Yorkshire Railway, backed by the Leeds & Bradford, was promoted to run from Bradford through Halifax to Sowerby Bridge in the Calder Valley. Here it would join

the Manchester & Leeds Railway which responded by sponsoring the Leeds & West Riding Junction Railway, a rival scheme involving a network of lines around the West Riding more fully described in the 'Calder Valley' book. Part of the project was an alternative to the West Yorkshire Railway. Linking Sowerby Bridge, Halifax, Bradford and Leeds, it differed from its rival by adopting the 'short line' between Bradford and Leeds via Stanningley.

The West Yorkshire and Leeds & West Riding Junction schemes both went before Parliament in 1845 and were both rejected. The Manchester & Leeds Railway then proposed amalgamation with the Leeds & Bradford. This offer was accepted by Hudson and a detailed agreement reached in November 1845. It was proposed that the link between Sowerby Bridge and Bradford would be built and the Leeds & Bradford Railway would then be part of the Manchester to Leeds main line.

The Midland Railway may have wondered what its chairman was doing giving the Leeds & Bradford line to a company which was outside the Hudson Empire and not on particularly good terms with the Midland. Hudson evidently had second thoughts and in June 1846 broke off the amalgamation, blaming the Manchester & Leeds for deviating from the agreed terms, and offered the Leeds & Bradford to the Midland Railway on terms which were excessive but benefited him personally. He then took the chair at a general meeting of Midland Railway shareholders and spoke and voted in favour of the deal.

This event marked the beginning of the decline of Hudson's power as his dealings began to come under closer scrutiny. It also condemned Bradford Midland

Station (the name Forster Square was not used until 1924) to remain a dead end with no connection to Bradford's other railways. The Manchester & Leeds Railway reached Bradford Exchange in 1850 but dropped plans to connect with the Leeds & Bradford line. Instead from 1854, its trains reached Leeds via the Leeds, Bradford & Halifax Junction Railway – the rival 'short line'.

Shipley to Skipton

Work on the line to Keighley and Skipton proceeded quickly and a locomotive was able to travel to Keighley on 13 February 1847. A Board of Trade inspection was carried out by Captain Simmons on 13 March and the public opening took place on Tuesday 16 March. Captain Simmons was back on 28 August as a single track was available between Keighley and Skipton. Following his approval and a directors special trip on 1 September, the line was opened to the public on Tuesday 7 September. By December, a second track was in use along with intermediate stations at Steeton, Kildwick and Cononley.

At this stage Skipton was a dead end but from 2 October 1848, the Midland Railway extended to Colne. On 1 February 1849, this town was also reached by the East Lancashire Railway from Burnley and from 2 April that year it became possible to get from Leeds to Liverpool via Skipton and Colne.

The 'Little' North Western Railway, soon to become part of the Midland, opened from Skipton to Clapham on 30 July 1849 and within a year the route to Lancaster and Morecambe was in use throughout. The line through Airedale became part of the Midland route to Scotland with the opening of the Clapham to Lowgill line on 1

October 1861. The Midland Railway's control over this route ended at Ingleton. Dissatisfaction at the handling of its traffic thence to Carlisle by the London & North Western Railway was a major factor in determining the Midland to construct the Settle & Carlisle line which finally opened to passenger traffic on 1 May 1876.

Early Schemes in Wharfedale

The River Wharfe is crossed at Arthington by the railway from Leeds to Harrogate. This line began life as the Leeds & Thirsk Railway which was incorporated in 1845 and opened in stages during 1848 and 1849.

In 1846, an Act was passed for a railway through Wharfedale itself. A company called the Lancashire & Yorkshire North Eastern Railway later changed its name to the 'Wharfdale' Railway (there was no e in Wharfedale at that time). The proposal had been to run from Skipton to York but the section east of Arthington was dropped at the Parliamentary stage. The 'Wharfdale' was to be leased to the Leeds & Thirsk and might have stood more chance of being built if it had stuck to that proposal. However the arrangement was broken off in November 1846 when a majority of 'Wharfdale' shareholders decided that they should take an independent course. At their half yearly meeting in Leeds on 23 February 1847, hopes were held of the line being opened concurrently with the Leeds & Thirsk. Such optimism proved unfounded. The 'Wharfdale' scheme was abandoned in 1852 after failing to get help from any of the established neighbouring railways.

In 1856, a fresh attempt was made by promoters of a Wharfedale Railway to gain the backing either of the

4-4-0 No 41196 negotiates the old platform 1 at Shipley on 5 October 1957 with a Bradford to Skipton train. With the introduction of longer passenger coaches, there was insufficient clearance for trains to pass in platforms 1 and 2, which had to be worked as if single track. *(J C W Halliday)*

Between Kirkstall and Armley, the "fast" lines crossed over the "slow" so that traffic from Bradford could have a non conflicting route into Leeds City. The 1964 photograph is taken from a diesel hauled express, heading towards Leeds on the "slow" line.
(Peter E Baughan)

Kirkstall being rebuilt in 1905 to accommodate four tracks.
(Martin Bairstow collection)

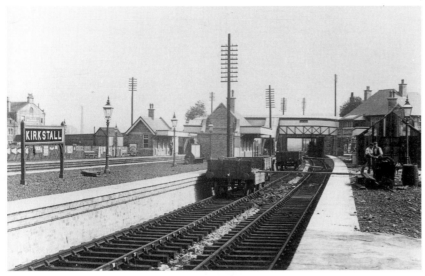

The remains of Kirkstall Forge Station, closed in 1905, could still be seen from a passing train in June 1964.
(Peter E Baughan)

Midland Railway or of the North Eastern (successor to the Leeds & Thirsk). Neither company was interested.

The Otley & Ilkley Joint Railway

During 1860 the Midland and North Eastern companies discussed the possibility of making a joint venture into Wharfedale, dispensing with any local promoters. The Midland was to build a branch from a junction near Apperley Bridge to Burley in Wharfedale, the North Eastern was to extend from Arthington to Otley and six miles of joint line were to link Otley and Ilkley. To conclude the agreement, the Midland undertook not to promote any new lines east of Otley and the North Eastern agreed not to do anything west of Ilkley. 11 July 1861 saw the passing of both the Midland and North Eastern Acts authorising their respective parts of the Otley & Ilkley Railway.

The town of Otley was en fête on 1 February 1865 when the first train arrived from Leeds at 7.38 am. Problems of land slips delayed the opening to Ilkley for a further six months. On 1 August both Midland and North Eastern trains began running into Ilkley to the accompaniment of brass bands.

At Arthington, the Otley and Ilkley line met the Leeds & Thirsk by a triangular junction. The station, which had previously been to the north of this point was resited with platforms on the Leeds – Otley and Leeds – Thirsk sides of the triangle. Another triangular layout was to be found between Menston, Burley and Milnerwood Junctions. The Burley to Milnerwood leg of this was part of the Otley & Ilkley Joint line but the other two curves were exclusively Midland property.

At Apperley Junction, the connection with the main line faced Leeds and it was necessary for trains from Bradford to reverse direction. The arrangements were anything but satisfactory and there was constant pressure voiced in the local press for a direct route from Bradford to Otley and Ilkley.

Problems at Apperley Viaduct

The embryonic Worth Valley line was not the only victim of the floods which hit West Yorkshire on 14 November 1866. The Midland Railway company was far more concerned with the destruction of Apperley Viaduct which severed Bradford, Skipton and all points north from the remainder of the Midland system.

A 'Bradford Observer' reporter travelled by the 1 pm train from Bradford to Otley. Instead of the 49 minutes allowed in the timetable the journey consumed three hours. The train had to make two attempts at the ascent from Apperley Junction to Guiseley. It eventually succeeded by the wrong line, the other track being blocked by an embankment slip. On the return journey the train got no further than Apperley Bridge station because that viaduct carrying the line over the River Aire had disappeared.

The Apperley Bridge station master was advised by the guard of the 4.50 pm Bradford to Leeds train that the viaduct appeared insecure. The station master set off on foot and was able to halt an up goods train. The driver of the train, which consisted of an engine, tender, two wagons and a guard's van, saw the station master's handlamp as he emerged from Thackley tunnel and brought the train to a stand on the viaduct. The level of the River Aire had risen considerably and was flowing through all ten arches of the viaduct instead of the usual three. According to a newspaper correspondent signing himself 'Eye witness' the train stood on the viaduct for fifteen minutes whilst the crew and the station master debated what to do. The decision was made for them when the viaduct collapsed. The engine and tender became embedded in the river whilst the van and wagons flowed downstream. Passengers who were stranded at Apperley Bridge must have faced a difficult journey home. The railway to Leeds was under three feet of water at Kirkstall whilst the road to Bradford was flooded where it crosses the River Aire below the station.

For the next week trains were terminated at Shipley and Apperley Bridge. Through passengers travelled by the Great Northern Railway from Leeds Central to Bradford Adolphus Street whence they walked to the Midland station. An editorial in the 'Bradford Observer' claimed that the Midland Railway had received just retribution for its failure to build a joint station in Bradford with the other railway companies. Various correspondents agreed and one, pursuing a similar theme, stated that the Midland Railway would have been spared the disruption to its traffic if it had built a proper route from Bradford to Ilkley as trains could have been diverted via Guiseley.

From 24 November trains reverted to the normal time-

Class G5 0 - 4 - 4T No 7240 approaching Otley with a train from Leeds to Ilkley on 11 June 1947.

(H C Casserley)

table but terminated at either side of Apperley Viaduct where passengers crossed a footbridge. A replacement viaduct was opened on 3 January 1867 only six weeks after the disaster occured.

Shipley to Guiseley

In order to offer a direct route between Bradford and Wharfedale, the Midland Railway obtained powers in 1872 for a 3½ mile double track line commencing at Guiseley Junction, near Shipley, and running over three viaducts and through three tunnels to reach Esholt Junction, near Guiseley.

The line, which opened on 4 December 1876 offered the most direct route between Harrogate and Bradford and running powers were granted to the North Eastern Railway from Milnerwood Junction to Bradford.

Shipley Station, looking towards Bradford, before the 1885 rebuilding which brought higher platforms, canopies and a subway as well as the single storey main building which is still in use today. Prior to 1849, the station had been a wooden structure south of Bradford Junction.
(Dorothy Burrows collection)

Ilkley to Skipton

Prompted possibly by local attempts to promote a link between Ilkley and Skipton, the Midland Railway assumed the initiative and obtained the necessary powers by an Act of 16 July 1883. Work started in April 1885 and it was possible to open as far as Bolton Abbey on 16 May 1888. The remaining six miles to Skipton opened on 1 October the same year.

Guiseley to Yeadon

In 1881 the promoters of a Leeds & Yeadon District Railway approached the North Eastern Railway with plans for a line from Headingley to Guiseley. Intermediate stations would serve Horsforth, Rawdon and Yeadon. The NER gave the stock answer that it could not support any new line in Wharfedale without the consent of the Midland Railway. The latter company sent its chairman and general manager to a public meeting at Yeadon Town Hall on 10 November 1883. They advised that if the project were restricted to a Guiseley to Yeadon branch, the Midland Railway would not oppose it and would be prepared to work the line on completion.

The Guiseley, Yeadon & Rawdon Act was passed on 16 July 1885. The necessary capital could not be raised locally and the company required a loan from the Midland

Railway. In 1893, the partially completed line was purchased by the Midland.

Goods traffic commenced on 26 February 1894. Although a passenger station was provided at Yeadon, no regular service ever operated but there were occasional excursions.

An extension was authorised in 1891 from Yeadon to join the NER by a flying junction north of Headingley but sufficient capital was not forthcoming and the project was abandoned.

The Bradford Through Line

In 1898 the Midland Railway embarked upon its West Riding Lines which were intended to bring its trains into Dewsbury, Huddersfield and Halifax. As explained in the 'Standedge' book, the link from the Midland Main Line at Royston to the Calder Valley near Horbury was opened in 1905 and Midland branches were built into Dewsbury and Huddersfield. These ended up as little more than goods sidings and the centre piece of the West Riding Lines was never built. This would have left the Lancashire & Yorkshire Railway in the Spen Valley between Cleckheaton and Low Moor, would have passed through a tunnel at Bowling then crossed the centre of Bradford on a viaduct. After serving high level platforms at Market Street (Forster Square) Station, it would have dropped down to the level of the existing railway before Manningham. The Midland would have exercised running powers between Horbury and Cleckheaton and would have been able to route some London to Scotland traffic via Bradford. The project was postponed on the outbreak of the First World War and never resumed.

From a 1911 calendar, a view of Forster Square as it would look in 1915 with a Midland train departing from the High Level station and passing in front of the Cathedral.
(Dorothy Burrows collection)

The Yeadon pick up goods passing through Guiseley Station with a modest pay load, during its last year of operation in 1964.

(D J Mitchell)

The pick up goods is ready to depart Yeadon, back to Guiseley about 1961.

(J C W Halliday)

Yeadon never had a regular passenger service but there were occasional excursions. 2 - 4 - 2T No 10634 and 0 - 6 - 0 No 3878 await departure for Blackpool on 21 August 1948.

(G H Butland)

Train Services

When the Leeds & Bradford line opened in 1846, the Midland Railway provided a passenger service at hourly intervals but reduced on Sundays. Most stopped at all intermediate stations as soon as these were open.

The timetable for November 1850 shows 14 weekday departures from Leeds and Bradford at hourly intervals from 7.00 am until 1.00 pm but less regular in the afternoon and evening. The journey time varies between 30 and 45 minutes and there are six trains on Sundays. From Bradford to Skipton there are eight trains each way (three Sundays) giving very tight connections at Shipley with the Leeds to Bradford trains. The 3.15 pm from Leeds calls only at Shipley where it allows one minute to change for Skipton which is reached non-stop at 4.08. The other trains stop at most or all stations giving an average Leeds – Skipton journey time of 1 hour 20 minutes.

The North Eastern Railway began to serve Otley in February 1865 with a service of six weekday trains each way from Leeds but with no Sunday trains. However this omission was rectified from 1 August when the service was extended to Ilkley with six trains on weekdays and four on Sundays taking a minimum of one hour for the journey.

From the same date the Midland Railway introduced five trains (three on Sundays) from both Leeds and Bradford to Otley and Ilkley. The through journey times were about one hour to Ilkley and 50 minutes to Otley. The method of working seems to have been for the train from Leeds to pause at Apperley Junction to attach the coaches from Bradford and then for the combined train to work to Guiseley where the various carriages were shunted into Ilkley and Otley portions. In the reverse direction, trains arrived at Guiseley from Ilkley and Otley. After shunting they proceeded with the Bradford coaches in the rear so that these could be detached at Apperley Junction.

When the Shipley to Guiseley line was opened in 1876, the working of Ilkley and Otley trains was improved and some ran as independent trains. But the practice remained of combining some and remarshalling them at Guiseley.

On 1 August 1877, the North Eastern Railway began a service, initially of three trains each weekday, from Harrogate to Bradford via Otley, Guiseley and Shipley.

A review of services shown in 'Bradshaw' for November 1880 shows the extent of developments which had then taken place. In the Aire Valley, the main emphasis is still on Leeds to Bradford and Bradford to Skipton services connecting at Shipley. The number of weekday Leeds to Bradford trains has risen to 36 with 13 on Sundays. The timetable is littered with complications and one wonders how the public or even railway staff were expected to understand it. The first train of the day is at 1.50 am from Leeds to Bradford which is the previous evening's 9.15 from St Pancras. This calls at Armley (by request), Apperley Bridge, Shipley and Manningham (by request). Then there is a 3.25 from Leeds which has mandatory calls at Apperley Bridge and Shipley but if you wanted to alight at Armley or Newlay, it would stop on informing the guard at Leeds. If you

"Jubilee" class No 45739 "Ulster" passing Guiseley Junction, Shipley in September 1958 with the "Waverley" to Edinburgh. The signal box on the right is Shipley Junction on the Great Northern line.
(Peter Sunderland)

Guiseley Station with Midland 2 - 4 - 0 No 1515 (later No 255) entering with a train for either Leeds or Bradford. The station buildings were demolished in the 1970s but the signal box survived until 1994 and is now at Bolton Abbey. The footbridge has been re erected at Kirkby Stephen.

(Martin Bairstow collection)

Ivatt 2 - 6 - 0 No 43113 leaving Skipton with ten coaches for Leeds in May 1959. The rear of the train is passing the pre 1876 station building.

(Peter Sunderland)

preferred to travel to Kirkstall, Calverley & Rodley or Manningham, it would stop but only if you were travelling through from a station south of Leeds. The first stopping train was at 5.00 from Leeds. Thereafter there was a mixture of fast, semi-fast and all stations trains spread rather unevenly through the day.

The first departure from Skipton was at 2.23 am. This train contained through coaches from Inverness, Aberdeen, Dundee, Edinburgh and Glasgow. It reached Leeds at 3.05 and was through to St Pancras. The only intermediate call in the Aire Valley was at Apperley Bridge. In order to provide Bradford connections into and out of this express, a train left Bradford at 2.25 and ran to Apperley Bridge and back calling at Shipley and, by request on the return journey only, at Manningham.

During the day there are 22 trains shown between Skipton and Bradford plus a few starting at Keighley. Nearly all have connections at Shipley for Leeds. In addition there are a few through services to Leeds afforded by trains from the Settle & Carlisle and Morecambe Lines.

In Wharfedale, the Midland Railway was still shunting some trains at Guiseley. There were eight each weekday from Leeds four of which ran independently and four of which still got tangled up with services from Bradford. Commuters from Bradford to Ilkley by the 5.50 pm completed their journey in 28 minutes which is faster than today's timing but with stops only at Burley and Ben Rhydding. Those lucky enough to finish work an hour earlier could catch the 4.50 which arrived at Ilkley at 5.21 with stops at Shipley (when required to take up passengers from Scotland for Ben Rhydding and Ilkley), Menston, Burley, Ben Rhydding and Ilkley. How often this Shipley stop was invoked and whether local passengers used to sneak in we have no record. The 12.37 and 2.25 pm from Ilkley to Leeds completed their journeys in 32 minutes with stops at Burley and Guiseley. Inevitably they also stopped at Ben Rhydding, 'when required to take up for Sheffield and stations south thereof.'

On Sundays, there was no service from Leeds into Wharfedale but a train left Bradford at 8.10 am and proceeded to Ilkley then on to Otley before returning to Bradford. The exercise was repeated at 6.50 pm but Otley was served before Ilkley.

The North Eastern Railway, which did not like running trains on Sundays, managed nine return workings each weekday between Leeds and Ilkley. The 1.35 pm from Leeds and 2.30 from Ilkley completed the journey in 38 minutes by running non-stop between Holbeck and Otley. There were four trains between Bradford Market Street and Harrogate serving Shipley, Guiseley and Otley with a journey time of 50-55 minutes.

In 1908, slip coaches were introduced on two southbound expresses passing Saltaire in the early evening. The rear coach was slipped and brought to a stand in Saltaire station where a locomotive was attached to take passengers from Scotland into Bradford calling at intermediate stations by request. This facility ended during the First World War.

The level of service which had developed by 1910 can be seen from a summary of departures from Bradford Market Street. On Monday to Fridays there were 38 trains to Leeds. The Midland Railway had 21 departures for the Otley and Ilkley line whilst the North Eastern offered nine

KEIGHLEY TO OXENHOPE

MIDLAND RAILWAY

WEEKDAYS	am	am	am	am	am	SO pm	SX pm	SO pm	pm	pm	SO pm	pm	SX pm	pm	pm	pm	pm	SO pm	SX pm	SO pm	pm
KEIGHLEY	5 25	7 33	8 06	9 10	11 18	12 20	1 00	1 05	1 55	2 50	3 37	4 48	5 35	6 10	6 57	7 52	8 55	9 45	10 10	10 50	11 35
INGROW	5 29	7 37	8 10	9 13	11 22	12 24	1 04	1 09	1 59	2 55	3 41	4 52	5 40	6 14	7 01	7 56	8 59	9 49	10 14	10 54	11 39
DAMEMS	5 32	7 40	—	—	11 25	12 27	1 07	1 12	2 02	2 58	3 44	4 55	5 43	6 17	—	7 59	9 02	9 52	10 17	10 57	—
OAKWORTH	5 35	7 43	8 14	9 18	11 28	12 30	1 10	1 15	2 05	3 01	3 47	4 58	5 46	6 20	7 06	8 02	9 05	9 56	10 20	11 00	11 43
HAWORTH	5 39	7 47	8 18	9 22	11 32	12 34	1 14	1 19	2 09	3 05	3 51	5 02	5 50	6 24	7 09	8 06	9 09	10 00	10 24	11 04	11 47
OXENHOPE	5 42	7 50	8 21	9 25	11 35	12 37	1 17	1 22	2 12	3 08	3 54	5 06	5 53	6 27	7 12	8 09	9 13	10 03	10 27	11 07	11 50

SUNDAYS	am	am	pm	pm	pm	pm	pm
KEIGHLEY	7 00	10 50	1 55	2 50	5 15	7 40	9 06
INGROW	7 04	10 54	1 59	2 54	5 19	7 44	9 10
DAMEMS	—	—	—	—	—	—	—
OAKWORTH	7 08	10 58	2 03	2 58	5 23	7 48	9 14
HAWORTH	7 12	11 02	2 07	3 02	5 27	7 52	9 18
OXENHOPE	7 15	11 06	2 11	3 06	5 31	7 56	9 21

WEEKDAYS	am	am	am	am	am	am	am	am	SO pm	pm	pm	SO pm	SX pm	pm	pm	SX pm	pm	pm	pm	pm	SO pm	SX pm	SO pm
OXENHOPE	5 07	5 48	6 53	7 55	8 26	9 32	10 50	11 40	12 43	1 30	2 18	3 13	3 25	4 03	5 12	5 57	6 35	7 17	8 18	9 20	10 10	10 32	11 13
HAWORTH	5 10	5 51	6 56	7 58	8 29	9 35	10 53	11 43	12 46	1 33	2 21	3 16	3 28	4 07	5 15	6 00	6 38	7 20	8 21	9 23	10 13	10 35	11 16
OAKWORTH	5 14	5 55	7 00	8 02	8 33	9 39	10 57	11 47	12 50	1 37	2 25	3 20	3 32	4 11	5 19	6 03	6 42	7 24	8 25	9 27	10 17	10 39	11 20
DAMEMS	—	5 58	7 03	—	8 36	—	11 00	—	12 53	—	2 28	—	3 35	4 15	5 22	—	6 45	—	8 28	9 30	10 20	10 42	11 23
INGROW	5 20	6 02	7 05	8 06	8 38	9 43	11 03	11 52	12 56	1 42	2 31	3 25	3 39	4 18	5 24	6 08	6 47	7 29	8 32	9 33	10 23	10 46	11 27
KEIGHLEY	5 24	6 06	7 11	8 10	8 43	9 47	11 06	11 55	1 00	1 45	2 35	3 29	3 42	4 22	5 30	6 12	6 52	7 32	8 35	9 36	10 27	10 49	11 30

SUNDAYS	am	pm	pm	pm	pm	pm	pm
OXENHOPE	7 25	12 25	2 20	3 55	6 50	8 02	9 26
HAWORTH	7 28	12 28	2 23	3 58	6 53	8 05	9 29
OAKWORTH	7 32	12 32	2 27	4 02	6 57	8 09	9 33
DAMEMS	7 35	—	—	4 05	—	—	—
INGROW	7 37	12 37	2 32	4 09	7 03	8 15	9 38
KEIGHLEY	7 43	12 41	2 35	4 12	7 07	8 18	9 41

SKIPTON TO GRASSINGTON & THRESHFIELD

MIDLAND RAILWAY

WEEKDAYS	am	am	SO pm	pm	pm	pm	pm	SUNDAYS am	SUNDAYS pm
SKIPTON	8 37	11 40	1 10	3 12	4 38	5 55	7 35	8 45	7 00
RYLSTONE	8 57	12 00	1 30	3 32	4 58	6 15	7 55	9 05	7 20
GRASSINGTON & T	9 05	12 08	1 38	3 40	5 06	6 23	8 03	9 13	7 28

WEEKDAYS	MO am	am	am	pm	pm	pm	pm	SUNDAYS am	SUNDAYS pm
GRASSINGTON & T	7 15	7 45	9 12	12 15	3 50	5 15	8 10	9 25	7 55
RYLSTONE	7 24	7 54	9 21	12 24	3 59	5 24	8 19	9 34	8 04
SKIPTON	7 41	8 14	9 38	12 41	4 16	5 42	8 36	9 52	8 21

MIDLAND TRAINS OTLEY TO ILKLEY

	WEEKDAYS	SUNDAYS
F on. OTLEY	7 19pm	8 59pm
From ILKLEY	8 45am	9 22am

LEEDS TO OTLEY AND ILKLEY

NORTH EASTERN RAILWAY

WEEKDAYS ONLY	am	am	am	am	am	pm	pm	pm	pm	pm	pm	pm	pm	pm
LEEDS NEW	7 43	7 55		9 24	11 48	1 23	3 00	5 00	5 30	8 13	9 10		10 10	
HOLBECK	7 47	7c59		9 28	11 52	1 27	3 05	5 05	5 34	8 18	9 15		10 15	
HEADINGLEY	7 53	—		9 34	11 58	—	—	5 11	—	8 24	9 22		10 22	
HORSFORTH	8 00	—		9 41	12 05	—	—	5 18	—	8 31	9 30		10 30	
ARTHINGTON	8 07	8 13	8 22	9 48	12 13	—	3 22	5 26	—	8 38	9 36	9 42	10 36	10 48
POOL IN W DALE	8 09		8 25	9 51	12 16	—	3 25	5 29	—	8 41		9 45		10 51
OTLEY			8 31	9 57	12 22	1 49	3 32	5 36	5 54	8 48		9 51		10 57
BURLEY IN W DALE			8 37	10 03	12 28	1 55	3 38	5 42	6 00	8 54		9 57		11 03
BEN RHYDDING			8 42	10 08	12 33	2 00	3 43	5 47	6 05	8 59		10 02		11 08
ILKLEY			8 45	10 11	12 36	2 03	3 46	5 50	6 08	9 02		10 05		11 11

WEEKDAYS ONLY	am	am	am	am	am	am	pm	pm	pm	pm	pm	pm	pm	pm
ILKLEY	7 25		8 17		9 00	10 45	12 50	2 16	4 00	6 15	8 25		10 05	
BEN RHYDDING	7 28		8 20		9 03	10 48	12 53	2 19	4 03	6 18	8 28		10 08	
BURLEY IN W DALE	7 33		8 25		9 08	10 53	12 59	2 24	4 08	6 23	8 33		10 13	
OTLEY	7 39		8 31		9 14	10 59	1 06	2 30	4 14	6 29	8 39		10 19	
POOL IN W DALE	7 45		—	8 40	9 20	11 05	1 12	—	4 21	6 35	8 45		10 25	
ARTHINGTON	7 48	7 51	—	8 44	9 23	11 08	1 16	2 36	4 24	6 38	8 48	9 02	10 28	10 44
HORSFORTH		8 00	—	8 52	—	11 16	1 25	2 44	4 32	6 46		9 12		10 54
HEADINGLEY		8 05	—	8 56	—	11 22	1 31	—	4 38	6 52		9 17		10 59
HOLBECK		8 11	8 52	9 01	9 39	11 30	1 38	2 54	4 44	7 00		9 23		11 05
LEEDS NEW		8 15	8 55	9 04	9 43	11 34	1 42	2 58	4 48	7 04		9 27		11 09

ILKLEY TO SKIPTON

MIDLAND RAILWAY

WEEKDAYS ONLY	cm	am	am	am	pm	pm	SO pm	pm	pm	SX pm	pm	pm	SO pm
ILKLEY	6 00	8 10	9 53	10 44	12 52	2 10	2 51	4 40	5 27	6 03	7 05	8 25	10 32
ADDINGHAM	6 07	8 17	10 00	10 51	12 59	2 17	2 58	4 47	5 34	6 10	7 12	8 32	10 38
BOLTON ABBEY	6 13	8 24	10 07	10 57	1 06	2 24	3 04	4 53	5 41	6 17	7 18	8 39	
EMBSAY		8 32	10 16		1 15	2 33			5 50	6 26	7 26	8 48	
SKIPTON		8 38	10 21		1 20	2 40			5 57	6 31	7 31	8 55	

WEEKDAYS ONLY	am	am	am	am	pm	pm	SO pm	SO pm	pm	pm	SO pm	pm	pm	SO pm
SKIPTON		7 05	8 22	10 48		1 33	2 00	3 45		5 40		7 43	9 15	
EMBSAY		7 13	8 30	10 56		1 41	2 08	3 53		5 50		7 51	9 23	
BOLTON ABBEY	6 22	7 21	8 38	11 04	12 45	1 49	2 16	4 01	5 40	5 58	7 12	7 59	9 31	
ADDINGHAM	6 29	7 28	8 45	11 11	12 52	1 56	2 23	4 08	5 47	6 05	7 19	8 06	9 38	10 50
ILKLEY	6 34	7 33	8 50	11 16	12 57	2 01	2 28	4 13	5 52	6 10	7 24	8 11	9 43	10 55

MO MONDAYS ONLY: SO SATURDAYS ONLY: SX SATURDAYS EXCEPTED: c WEDNESDAYS AND THURSDAYS ONLY

APRIL 1910

Class 1P 0 - 4 - 4T No 1407 approaching Esholt with a Bradford Forster Square to Ilkley local on 25 September 1937. *(G H Butland)*

NER class U (later G5) 0 - 4 - 4T No 1888 in platform 1 at Ilkley with a train for Leeds via Otley.
(Dorothy Burrows collection)

Sentinel railcar No 2133 "Cleveland" leaving Leeds for Ilkley via Otley on 1 August 1936. Leeds Neville Hill Shed had one diagram for a steam railcar, which visited Ilkley three times in the course of a long day involving trips also to Harrogate, South Milford and Wetherby.

(G H Butland)

semi fast trains to Harrogate. 28 trains left Bradford for Skipton or beyond with 12 more terminating at Keighley and another two at Bingley. This gave a total of 110 passenger trains in the 24 hours between Bradford and Shipley. With parcels, freight and light engine movements, the quadruple track was fully utilised.

Apart from temporary restrictions during the First World War which were restored soon afterwards, the pattern of train services established by the early part of the twentieth century remained largely unaltered until 1939.

The Second World War caused a significant reduction particularly at off peak times and, on many lines, passengers continued to be offered austerity level of service long after the cessation of hostilities.

'Bradshaw' for April 1957 shows the pattern of service which was by then so hopelessly inadequate to meet the onslaught of road competition. The number of Leeds to Bradford and Bradford to Skipton locals was about half the pre war level with huge gaps in the day time but an almost respectable service in the evening. Taking departures from Apperley Bridge to Leeds, these were at 6.59, 8.10, 8.38, 13.31, 16.04, 17.25, 18.25, 20.16, 21.10, 21.38 and 22.27. No trains called on Sundays.

Bradford to Ilkley had sunk even further with Monday to Friday departures at 7.48, 12.38, 16.22, 17.00, 17.33, 17.53 and 22.20. The timetable shows just one train to Otley and Harrogate at 17.15 from Forster Square but this had, in fact, been withdrawn from the previous 25 February. There were just four trains between Leeds and Ilkley via Otley but the service via Guiseley had held up rather better with nine. There were five trains between Ilkley and Skipton.

Change was at hand.

Pool in Wharfedale finished up with only three trains one way and two the other. There was still a bit of coal traffic in the yard when No 3442 "The Great Marquess" visited in May 1963.   *(D J Mitchell)*

The Coming of the Diesels

Nowadays, public transport has to be comfortable and it has to be speedy. The new diesel trains, with their pleasing interior fittings and clean, up to date furnishings, meet up with every requirement, so that more and more people are finding them a popular way of travel. - BR Publicity

I can certainly remember people talking about going to school or work "on the diesel" rather than "on the train". For a time, the North Eastern Region timetable carried a symbol to identify the diesel trains. It was a tragedy that the optimism of dieselisation in 1959, gave way so quickly to the despair of the Beeching Report only four years later.

The first timetabled incursion by diesel multiple units came on Summer Sundays in 1957 when an hourly service was introduced between Leeds Central and Ilkley via Otley. Most of the workings were through from Castleford via the Methley Joint, hence the use of Leeds Central. Three trains were extended to Bolton Abbey.

A radical new timetable was introduced on 5 January 1959 when nearly all local workings were taken over by DMUs operating at hourly intervals, with rush hour extras, on four routes: Leeds to Ilkley, Bradford to Ilkley, Leeds to Bradford and Bradford to Skipton. The latter two services connected at Shipley. There was no direct stopping service between Leeds and Skipton though there were a variety of through express and semi fast trains at irregular intervals.

Four of the Leeds - Ilkley trains went via Otley, the remainder via Guiseley. Five trains were extended through from Ilkley to Skipton. A handful of local trains continued with steam haulage because of the volume of parcels. Longer distance steam trains continued as before, including those between Bradford, Shipley and Leeds.

Overall, the number of trains was increased whilst journey times were reduced.

The hourly pattern also applied on a Sunday, though some of the intermediate stations were closed and others open only for the 12 weeks of the Summer timetable. The Wharfedale Line was served on Sundays only in Summer with hourly trains from both Leeds and Bradford to Bolton Abbey. In 1960, the Leeds trains were transferred from Central via Otley to City via Guiseley. For that season only, Otley was compensated with a Sunday diesel service from Bradford Forster Square to Harrogate and Knaresborough.

The Crumbling Edge of Quality

At first the entire service stuck very close to the regular interval pattern. Almost all local trains stopped at every station, except for those, which were closed on Sundays. Gradually, cracks began to

During the first week of diesel operation, in January 1959, one of the new Derby built units, later class 108, waits in the bay platform at Keighley.

(Peter Sunderland)

A Skipton to Bradford DMU calls at Bolton Abbey in February 1965.

(D J Mitchell)

appear at the edges. Largely, this involved eliminating odd station stops, sometimes for no obvious reason, but often to permit stations to close earlier in the evening. After September 1963, the last train to stop at Frizinghall was the 7.41pm to Leeds. From September 1964, evening trains were withdrawn between Bradford and Ilkley after the 6.50 departure, 6.30pm the other way.

At Apperley Bridge, the Station Master, Mr Carr actually requested that the last two pairs of trains should no longer stop. His wish was granted from June 1964, after Divisional Office had first pointed out the damaging effect this would have on passengers returning from day trips to certain destinations. Mr Carr's response was to say that nobody made such journeys anymore.

I can remember Mr Carr expressing, to my Father, fear for his livelihood if the station closed, concern that his son might have to leave Woodhouse Grove School. Was this apparently suicidal act some kind of vain attempt to save the station by reducing the wage bill? Or was it, as Leading Porter Melvin Marsh suggested, that he wanted the overtime but not too much of it? By 1964, they were not filling vacancies. When there was no late turn leading porter, Melvin would work 12 hours from 6.30am to 6.30pm and the Station Master would then cover until the last train, just after 9pm, previously two hours longer.

A leading porter was one passed out on tickets. When there was no clerk on duty, he would man the booking office. Except when the signal box was switched out, the impending arrival of a stopping train was announced on the platform bell, which repeated in the booking office. The incumbent would then lock the office, proceed to the platform, call out the station name, collect tickets from alighting passengers, assist those who needed help with the low platforms and deal with the loading and unloading of parcels.

It was the parcels business, which kept station staff occupied. Gradually, they were rationalising the number of stations, which performed this function. Apperley Bridge retained a delivery area to the end. On the very last day, arriving parcels were put on trains back to Leeds with instruction that they be redirected to Guiseley. At Frizinghall, staff rarely attended the arrival of trains, especially on the Bradford platform, which was furthest from the office. At Calverley & Rodley, the incumbent might consider that he had "seen out" the train if he tapped on a window from the footbridge. Those who lament the days when travellers had the comfort and assurance of stations manned at all times are really mistaken as to the reality. The booking office window firmly shut with a hand written note saying "please knock". You might do that in vain if the occupant was next door in the "Railway Tavern"

Yet, at least in part, it was the cost of providing this "attendance" which was threatening the survival of these stations. Oxenhope became unstaffed from 1955 and was later joined by Ingrow, the guard issuing tickets from a setright machine. Elsewhere by the early 1960s, Addingham had no late turn staff. Headingley and Arthington were unattended in the evening. These situations were so noteworthy that they were detailed in the timetable

The Creaking Fabric

The diesel trains were new. The permanent way and signalling had to be maintained. The stations, however, could go to rack and ruin - as long as they didn't fall onto the tracks.

At Frizinghall, the main building on the road bridge was demolished about 1958. The ticket office was transferred to a former waiting room on the up platform. About the same time, the platform canopies were removed at Apperley Bridge. The two wooden staircases were exposed to the elements

By 1958, the canopies and awnings at Apperley Bridge were in need of repair. Instead, they were demolished. After this, no buildings remained at all on platform 4, the original up slow line platform, which was not rebuilt at the 1900 widening. *(J C W Halliday)*

and all buildings were demolished on platform 4, which had survived the 1900 rebuilding. Access to this platform was by a stone staircase. At night you had to stamp your feet to make the gas lamp burn brighter in order to find your way down. Some of the lamps needed to be switched on in a particular order or they wouldn't light at all. They had pilot lights and were operated by pulling short chains. As these were mostly out of arm's reach, one used a metal rod with a hook on the end.

The lights had to be cleaned regularly and the mantles changed. Gradually, as morale sank, staff would allow those at the farthest end of the platforms to become derelict, or decapitated. I remember Menston as one of the few stations, which still bothered illuminating the full platform lengths.

In an age when we took domestic electricity for granted, nearly all the stations were gas lit. Only Bradford Forster Square had fluorescent tubes. Keighley and Armley Canal Road had electric bulbs hanging on the old gas columns.

The first time I travelled from Skipton to Ilkley, in late 1963, after dark, the lamps at Embsay and

Bolton Abbey seemed very dim. It was only when we pulled into Addingham, dazzling by contrast, that I realised the wonders of gas lighting had not yet reached every station. Arthington and Pool in Wharfedale also relied on oil lanterns.

At Saltaire, the original paved platforms were low requiring a porter to manhandle wooden steps to assist passengers boarding and alighting. There were wooden platform extensions, of the same inadequate height, extending towards Bingley. Provided for long excursion trains, these were removed shortly before the station closed in 1965. Platform 4 at Apperley Bridge was of similar standard and construction. Even platform 1, built for the widening in 1900, required steps for all but the most agile. Possibly, the cant on the track had been increased over the years. At Manningham, the porter lifted my Grannie off the train, commenting that she was so light, it wasn't worth fetching the steps. Platform 3 at Ilkley was bad. It was the opposite face of platform 2 but, whilst the terminal track was level, the "down" Skipton line was on a rising gradient.

An attraction of the first generation DMUs was the forward view available to passengers. Approaching Otley on 10 March 1965.
(Geoffrey Lewthwaite)

Inside the booking office at Pool in Wharfedale on the final day, 20 March 1965. The small ticket rack is to the right of the closed hatch or window. The safe is below the cash draw is in the middle of the counter. The position of the date stamp assumes staff to be right handed. Scissors are in easy reach for cutting tickets in half for children.
(John Holroyd)

The Sharpening of the Axe

Some of the threatened services did indeed convey minimal traffic. That is not to say they wouldn't have been doing a lot more today. A Bradford to Skipton DMU calls at Addingham early in 1965.

(D J Mitchell)

The diesels had transformed the passenger service. They had also done something to improve rolling stock utilisation and train crew productivity. But in other respects, they had just been superimposed on a system, which was still living in the Edwardian era.

Even as they proclaimed the success of their diesel program, BR managers were already engaged on collating data for the Beeching Report, which was published in March 1963.

I don't suppose many people have actually read the Report. Yet few will have escaped its main conclusion / recommendation. Whether by accident or design, for it was without the aid of media consultants, Dr Beeching got across the message that a large part of the network carried only a tiny proportion of the traffic, was unprofitable and should be eliminated. This is a gross oversimplification, both of the Report itself and of the underlying problem. But why bother with technicality when the headline story was doing so well.

The almost universal acceptance of the Beeching Report was a remarkable achievement. As recently as February 1963, *Modern Railways* had been predicting that the Report would never get published because of the likely electoral consequence of a program of widespread closures. Yet it was published, to widespread acclaim. Within months, it began to be implemented.

Something, which might have blown the plan off course, would have been the continued pursuit of greater efficiency in operating local passenger trains. Dieselisation needed to be accompanied by reductions in station staff, automation of level crossings and rationalisation of track and signalling. As recalled in *Railways in East Yorkshire*, steps in this direction were beginning to happen on the lines from Hull to Hornsea, Withernsea and York. They were stopped. Once it became accepted that cost reductions were possible, as an alternative to closure, then the whole program could have been thrown into doubt. Public opinion might have swung against closing even the most hopeless cases.

Under Beeching, the official line was that diesel schemes had not been the success previously claimed and that cost reductions, such as destaffing stations, were either impractical or insufficient to have any impact. The DMU building program had stopped at the end of 1961. Further replacement of steam trains by these vehicles would have to come from closing existing diesel services.

Nothing had to stand in the way of implementing the plan, unless the Government were to reprieve individual lines or stations, possibly on a temporary basis, for some social or political reason. In the first three years, post 1963, such reprieves were few in number.

The Railway delivery service was a very familiar sight up to the 1960s. It didn't disappear completely until 1981. The Bradford Forster Square fleet includes a Scammell "mechanical horse". *(J C W Halliday)*

After the closures of 1965 and 1967, only two platforms remained in use for passengers at Bradford Forster Square. The rest of the station was the sole preserve of the still significant parcels trade. A class 104 for Ilkley and a 108 for Keighley on 27 April 1974. *(Tom Heavyside)*

The Beeching Report recommended closure of all lines in Wharfedale, most stations in Airedale and Bradford Forster Square. A "modified" service was to continue between Leeds, Skipton and Morecambe. Freight closures were expected to accompany passenger withdrawals but it was the latter only which were subject to any consultative process.

A formal closure proposal was issued in October 1963, seeking to implement the entire Beeching Report in Airedale and Wharfedale, apart from Bradford Forster Square which, for the time being, would retain its steam hauled expresses to Leeds and beyond, also a "feeder" DMU as far as Keighley.

It was clear, both from the Press and from documentation sent to objectors, that the plight of stations Guiseley to Ilkley stood out very differently to the others. The Ilkley Railway Supporters Association made a well organised case. In stark contrast, I remember the pathetic petition posted outside the booking office at Frizinghall. There wasn't even space for signatories to put their address. Even at age 11, I knew that a petition was supposed to show full name and address as well as signature.

Ten names on the list of "official objectors" came from addresses at Apperley Bridge. I was one of them. Three were parcels customers. One was the Headmaster of Woodhouse Grove School, which had by far the greatest ground for objection. As far as I know, he or a representative attended the subsequent public hearing in Ilkley but either didn't, or was not allowed to, speak.

The effort of Bradford Grammar School, at Frizinghall, was just as token. Thinking of the Settle - Carlisle campaign 20 years later, they could have got every pupil to write an individual objection, sent pro formas for parents to fill in and put out regular press statements. Anything to swing the balance of political expediency in favour of a token reprieve. In the 1960s, these institutions still upheld the tradition that you didn't argue with authority or assume ideas above, or even concerning, your station.

Aside from the main Ilkley campaign, there were pleas from isolated communities at Arthington and Cononley, complaints that Samuel Ledgard buses lacked heaters and the inevitable claims that stations should remain open as unstaffed halts. This point was made at Arthington, which c ould still have the Harrogate trains, even if the Otley line closed. The BR answer was that "this particular station produces a safety problem". Apparently, without staff in attendance, mothers with prams would be tempted to use the sleeper crossing rather than the subway between platforms and would not be able to see oncoming trains emerging from Bramhope Tunnel.

The weakness in this argument was that the station already was unstaffed in an evening, when passengers with or without prams had to fend for themselves, guided only by dim oil lighting.

These proceedings were not tribunals. Evidence was not subject to scrutiny. The outcome lay with the Minister of Transport, Ernest Marples, the political architect of the Beeching Report. By September 1964, he or his civil servants were in a hurry. The Minister was about to go off and fight an election from which he might not return. They had to get his signature to as many closure cases as possible. On 11 September, 41 closure decisions were announced, nearly all of them adverse. No part of the Airedale and Wharfedale proposal was actually refused but a decision was deferred in respect of the main Ilkley service. The weight of genuine evidence in favour of Ilkley was too great to be rushed through before the election.

The weekend of 20 / 21 March saw the end of passenger service between Arthington and Burley in Wharfedale, from Ilkley to Skipton and at all the

A Stanier 2 - 6 - 2 tank draws into Ben Rhydding with a train for Leeds via Guiseley on 2 January 1959.

(J C W Halliday)

Demolition at Pool in Wharfedale during Summer 1966. The site is now a housing estate, whence commuters battle it into Leeds by car. *(J C W Halliday)*

smaller stations between Leeds, Bradford and Skipton. An approx hourly DMU service was introduced between Leeds and Skipton with some workings through to Morecambe in place of the previous steam trains. Most of these stopped at Shipley, despite the absence of main line platforms. Leeds - Ilkley and Bradford - Ilkley trains continued more or less as before, including Summer Sundays. An irregular service of ten trains per day ran between Bradford Forster Square and Keighley.

Remaining goods traffic was soon withdrawn from the sections closed to passengers. The yards at Otley, Pool and Addingham closed on 3 July 1965. Bolton Abbey had already closed. The only regular through train, the Billingham to Heysham oil tanks, was rerouted via Leeds. This allowed the line through Otley to close completely and left Ilkley to Embsay without any booked traffic. This stretch remained available for diversions, the last of which took place on 24 October 1965. It was closed on the first weekend of 1966. Embsay remained open for quarry traffic until October 1968.

May 1967 saw the withdrawal of remaining through passenger trains between Leeds and Bradford Forster Square, where passenger facilities were reduced to just two platforms for the trains to Ilkley and Keighley. The other four were given over to the exclusive use of parcels, which was still a significant operation.

Threat of Complete Closure

We were now four years on from the Beeching Report. A high proportion of the planned closures had been carried out. In round figures, the BR network had shrunk from about 20,000 miles to 12,000. The Beeching Report would have reduced it to 8,000 but there seemed no stomach for some of the more contentious closures. Still less, did it seem that "Beeching Part Two" was going to be adopted. Published in 1965, there was doubt whether this really was a proposal to reduce the network to 3,500 miles or whether it was just a plan to concentrate investment on those routes "selected for development".

By 1967, things were beginning to change. To the disappointment of many railwaymen, the 1964 Labour Government had continued approving closures at the same 40 a month rate as Marples. At the end of 1965, a new Transport Minister was appointed, Barbara Castle. Alongside Marples, she was alone amongst countless holders of this post not to have been an extreme "lightweight". She signalled a slowing down in the pace of closures and proposed a system of Government support to sustain a network of around 11,000 miles. She published a White Paper, complete with map identifying this "basic" network. Leeds - Skipton - Morecambe was one of the few routes included in Beeching's 8,000 miles which failed to find a place in

The human, but unsustainable, face of the pre Beeching railway. Guard and porter exchange pleasantries at Arthington on 2 January 1959. Was it the method of operation or the very existence of the Railway, which needed to be addressed?

(J C W Halliday)

In pre Beeching times, many closed stations lay dormant, still available for parcels and excursion traffic. But not under the new regime. A rare exception was this Sunday School trip, which called at Kirkstall on 3 July 1965. It had probably been arranged prior to closure on 20 March and the booking was honoured for this occasion only.

(Geoffrey Lewthwaite)

Closure was quickly followed by demolition. 8F 2 - 8 - 0 No 48352 in charge of the track lifting train at Otley on 23 June 1966. *(G W Morrison)*

Castle's 11,000. It was possibly tied up with the continuing quest for electrification from Crewe; to Glasgow. BR was trying to "buy" Government approval with a promise to sacrifice the entire Midland network, North of Leeds.

The promise of the White Paper was for no railways at all in Airedale and Wharfedale.

In Summer 1968, it was finally announced that the Minister of Transport would not proceed with the still deferred Ilkley decision. Instead, he instructed BR to restart the statutory procedure, this time to include closure of Bradford Forster Square in the proposal. Bradford Corporation opposed the closure. Leeds declined even to submit a simple written objection, explaining that they could find no grounds upon which to object. The ensuing public hearing brought the Ilkley Railway Supporters Association back into action. The number of written objections was greater than before. By then a 16 year old, I managed to submit six of them - all genuine. I mobilised my Grannie and some of her friends.

Continuing Uncertainty

On 5 October 1968, Ilkley and the other branch stations issued their last tickets. Through bookings to or from anywhere beyond Bradford or Leeds were abolished and flimsy paper tickets, singles only, were issued by the guard on the train. Even passengers joining at Leeds were unable to buy tickets for Ilkley except on the train. This "paytrain" arrangement persisted until well into the 1980s. In an attempt to be seen to be saving money, the stations became unstaffed, at least as regards serving passengers. In truth, Guiseley retained staff until the parcels business finished. Ilkley was manned throughout its 29 years as an unstaffed halt. Until 1988, the incumbent switched on the gas lights manually.

It took until August 1972 to get a Ministerial decision on the closure question. This, when it finally came, was a strange compromise, fortunately never implemented. The Leeds - Ilkley service won another reprieve but Bradford to Keighley was condemned. Bradford to Ilkley was to be reduced in frequency and sent by the pre 1876 route, with reversal at Apperley Junction.

This announcement came less than two years before local government reorganisation, which would see creation of the West Yorkshire Passenger Transport Executive. Bradford Corporation took the view that the direct Shipley to Guiseley route must not be destroyed, at least until the PTE had a chance to consider its long term potential. In a move then without precedent, they offered a subsidy to keep both the Ilkley and Keighley services as they were. They invited, and received, financial contributions from the small authorities who would soon merge into the Metropolitan District of Bradford : Shipley, Bingley, Keighley, Baildon and Ilkley. At that time, the City of Bradford extended only as far as Frizinghall. Bradford Corporation did not want the principal towns of the future Metropolitan District to have trains to Leeds but not to Bradford itself. The offer was accepted and the service continued unchanged.

Baildon Urban District Council contributed its share of the subsidy, even though it derived no benefit from the service. Immediately, it offered to meet the £2,500 cost of restoring Baildon Station, at which all trains called from 5 January 1973.

Reopening Baildon was a significant move. Up to that time, station reopenings, even as unstaffed halts, had been extremely rare. The modest cost, about £20,000 in today's money, was helped by the platforms still being in situ. Those at Frizinghall had been demolished only in 1972. Three years later, reopening fell through due to the cost of rebuilding. Nowadays, the price of a two platform unstaffed halt is quoted at up to £2m.

156 486 deposits passengers from Bradford at Baildon about 1997. Despite electrification, there remain plenty of diesel workings. The Settle & Carlisle style building has not been in railway use since the 1953 closure. The track was singled in 1983.
(Martin Bairstow)

The West Yorkshire PTE

The PTE has reversed many of the 1960s closures and seeks to do more. 144.002 calls at Saltaire, with a Skipton to Leeds service on 10 February 1991.   *(Martin Bairstow)*

The first Passenger Transport Executives were set up under the Transport Act, 1968. The idea was that in four, later seven, most densly populated conurbations, the task of co - ordinating road and rail transport should be given to these bodies, which were a joint committee of the relevant local authorities. Between 1974 and 1986, they were a function of the Metropolitan County Councils. As regards rail services, the PTEs took over from Central Government responsibility for subsidising or closing them. The PTEs were given a Government grant, which was supposed to be phased out over a period. Cynics said that the Government was just transferring the unpalatable job of closing lines, which it hadn't the nerve to close itself.

The cynics were proved wrong. With very few minor exceptions, the story of railways under the PTE regime has been one of revival and development.

The West Yorkshire PTE was formed on 1 April 1974. It inherited an assortment of rail services, which had never been planned as a network but just happened to be what was left when the closure process slowed down.

The first physical evidence of PTE influence came in 1975 when platform levels were raised and electric lighting installed at Guiseley, Menston,

Burley and BenRhydding. Since destaffing, these stations had become very unsightly. Except at Menston, the remaining buildings were demolished and replaced by simple shelters. In May 1978, trains to Ilkley were put back onto an hourly interval from both Leeds and Bradford. Previously, the times had got increasingly erratic. A year later, the poorly patronised Bradford to Keighley service was increased at least threefold to a half hourly interval. At the time, this seemed an odd priority. Hourly Bradford - Skipton would have made more sense but would have crossed the PTE boundary, where the extra subsidy stopped.

1982 saw a new station built at Crossflatts. The Midland Railway had resisted requests for a station here, claiming it was too near to Bingley. Initial patronage suggested that the Midland may have been right and the PTE wrong. A large car park was opened there in the late 1990s to try and capture "park & ride" traffic. Saltaire reopened in 1984 and was far more successful. These two stations were unstaffed on a line which was not a "Paytrain" route". At first, patrons were sold tickets by the guard from an excess fares book. Soon, all lines were put on the same basis. If joining at a staffed station, you bought a ticket there. Otherwise, you could buy a ticket on the train to anywhere on the BR

Steeton & Silsden has proved one of the most successful PTE initiatives, attracting park & ride traffic from quite a radius. 144 004 restarts for Skipton on 3 June 1990, shortly after the station reopened.

(Martin Bairstow)

In 1990, Bradford Forster Square was moved, largely to make way for property development. A 142 uses the incomplete new station, whilst the old awaits demolition.

(Martin Bairstow)

network. The guards, now restyled conductors, carried more sophisticated ticket machines and fares manuals.

1985 brought a temporary setback. From 30 September, the through service from Bradford to Ilkley was reduced to just three rush hour workings. At other times, there was an hourly train from Bradford to Guiseley, where passengers had to change on to the Leeds - Ilkley train. At the same time, the Bradford to Keighley service was halved to hourly.

The reduced timetable permitted closure of Burley Junction Box, which despite its name, had existed for the previous 20 years solely to split the block section between Guiseley and Ilkley. It had five signals, the last semaphores in Wharfedale but no points. Its Midland Railway bells and block instruments lasted to the end. Our contributor, Bill Smith had moved from Embsay to Burley Junction in January 1965, when it was still a junction. On closure of Burley box, he moved to Ilkley where, at first, he handled only one train an hour from a small colour light switch console. Over the next few years, he found himself signalling up to three times as many trains. He retired in 1994 when Ilkley Box was demolished to make way for an even more dramatic development.

The PTE blamed the 1985 cutback on financial constraints imposed upon them by the Government. They threatened, or promised, that things would get even worse when the Metropolitan County Council was abolished in 1986.

However, the PTE continued from 1 April 1986 as a joint board of the five district councils in West Yorkshire. Almost immediately, it published a new "rail plan" under which all lines in West Yorkshire were secure. The cuts were quickly restored. Then services were enhanced, leading to the announcement in 1990 that the Airedale and Wharfedale lines were to be electrified.

"Pacer" units of class 142 and 144 began to appear late in 1986. Over the next few months they replaced the first generation DMUs on virtually all local trains. 7 September 1987 saw Frizinghall reopen. The PTE said they would be watching closely the performance of a station so close in to Bradford. Generally, it is the outer suburban stations, which generate worthwhile traffic. From observation, Frizinghall would do little, were it not for my former school. In 1997, the School Magazine reported that some 227 pupils were arriving at Frizinghall on Ilkley and Skipton trains plus one from Leeds. This is a higher figure than in my time, before closure. There may well be more of them living in Airedale and Wharfedale than there used to be.

May 1988 saw the hourly Bradford - Ilkley trains restored and Bradford - Keighley extended to Skipton. At the same time, Leeds - Skipton was increased to half hourly. A year later, Leeds - Ilkley went up to half hourly on Saturdays and from May 1990 on Mondays to Fridays as well. This required the Guiseley to Ilkley block section again to be split. Intermediate signals were installed at Burley, controlled from Guiseley box.

Cononley Station, outside the PTE area, reopened in 1988. The platforms here had never been removed. At much greater expense, Steeton & Silsden reopened in 1990. Work, which included a large car park, coincided with the opening of a new bypass road. This swept away the level crossing and signal box, although the latter was used as a taxi office for a time.

The number of longer distance trains increased in September 1988 with the rerouting to Bradford Forster Square of the remaining two or three through London trains, which had still been using Bradford Exchange. The following year's reprieve of the Settle & Carlisle Line secured the Leeds - Carlisle trains, whose numbers had risen to six per day from the low of two which had been reached in 1982. These stopped at Shipley, and Keighley. Bingley stops were added later.

144 012 negotiating the then platform 5 at Shipley "wrong line" with a Skipton to Leeds working on 8 September 1990.

The original "north curve", of 1848, was on a much tighter alignment with a 10mph restriction running through what is now the car park. It was replaced by the present 20mph curve on 20 June 1883. There was no platform until 1979   *(Martin Bairstow)*

Electrification

333 007 at Skipton in 2001. The sets have since been built up to four coaches.   *(Stuart Baker)*

Considering how little electrification has been carried out in this Country in recent years, the Airedale & Wharfedale scheme is quite remarkable. At 42 route miles, it is the largest project since electrification of the East Coast Main Line was completed in 1991.

I describe the scheme in the present tense because it is still incomplete pending delivery of the remaining centre cars for the class 333 Electric Multiple Units.

The forces behind electrification were two fold. First, Bradford Council was very keen to see that the East Coast scheme did not end in Leeds. The Council had been, and still is, protesting about the small number of through London trains, ever since the majority of them were withdrawn in 1971. Extending the electrification would, they reasoned (wrongly), cause more London trains to run through. They even spoke of Forster Square becoming a terminus for through trains to the Continent. Bradford had influence on the PTE, obviously. For a brief period in the late 1980s, it also had influence over Government. As the only Conservative controlled Metropolitan authority, it was favoured by Mrs Thatcher.

The PTE was persuaded in favour of electrification by the difficulty of obtaining new diesel stock. In 1988 they bought seven class 155s for the Calder Valley, an add on to a BR order for 35. They were so pleased with them that they asked Leyland to quote for ten more. The manufacturer declined. Instead, the PTE ventured up market and bought the ten class 158/9 units as an add on to the substantial order which BR had placed with BREL. The PTE were assured that, once the 158 order was finished, there would be no further opportunities to tag on to any orders for Diesel Multiple Units. This proved to be true for about ten years.

By contrast, the PTE was led to believe that electric trains would present no procurement problem as various parts of BR would be requiring them in large numbers over the next few years.

Passenger traffic on the Airedale and Wharfedale lines had doubled during the 1980s The PTE and Bradford Council argued that expenditure on electrification would avoid the need to spend considerably more on an Aire Valley motorway, plans for which had already threatened to demolish the newly rebuilt Saltaire Station and much of the village as well.

At Baildon, the track had been singled ten years earlier so, to electrify through the tunnels, they slewed the remaining track into the centre of the formation. A class 308 leaves for Ilkley on 30 December 2000, a day when the service all but broke down due to over-running engineering work at Leeds.

(Martin Bairstow)

The class 308s never provided a full service, leaving at least three diagrams daily to be covered by diesels. The situation still continues with the 333s.150 274 and 308 152 at Bradford Forster Square on 1 May 2000.

(Martin Bairstow)

In April 1990, the scheme won conditional approval from the Government. The start of work had to be delayed, and there was no provision for rolling stock. In July 1991, *Modern Railways* reported that the scheme was in jeapody. Without a decision on rolling stock, they would lose the chance of adding on to the order for class 323 units, which were being built for Greater Manchester and the West Midlands. So the cost would go up. If infrastructure work did not start soon, the plant and workforce from the East Coast Main Line would be dispersed so that side of the cost would rise as well. Then the scheme would fail the viability test against which it had been approved.

Infrastructure work began in 1992, after the Government had authorised the PTE to lease new rolling stock. But no Bank would take on the deal. They said that, under rail privatisation, a future operator might get hold of old rolling stock leaving the new fleet to stand idle. The PTE refused to guarantee payment in that scenario and the Government declined to rule out that the situation could happen. Hunslet, manufacturer of the class 323, kept the option open as long as it could but, in July 1992, the PTE cancelled the order. BR offered a fleet of class 308s to keep the project alive. Built in 1957, these were due for replacement on routes out of London Liverpool Street and would otherwise have been scrapped.

The first visible evidence of change came in Summer 1992 with opening of the up main line platform at Shipley. This avoided "wrong line" working and increased line capacity. The new platform became No 1. At the same time, 2 and 5 exchanged numbers.

For six weeks overlapping August 1992, the Ilkley line was closed for major work, including lowering the track through Greenbottom Tunnel, south of Guiseley. Our friend Bill Smith had a fairly easy time with no trains to signal at Ilkley. He and his mate had to visit both Ilkley and Guiseley boxes each day, using the replacement bus service, just to sign the train register to confirm that the boxes were still in working order. At that time, Guiseley box was staffed by relief men so there was nobody needing redeployment there. At first, the track at Guiseley was put back in its 1983 layout. During 1994, conventional double line was restored from Guiseley, through Esholt Junction and a little way along the Leeds line to a point now known as Springs Junction. The Bradford line branches off at Esholt Junction and is single line throughout to what is now called Dockfield Junction, the old Guiseley Junction, near Shipley. Another capacity improvement came at Skipton where track was restored in the old bay platform 1.

Electrification was accompanied by resignalling and a modest expansion of the infrastructure including the new platform 1 and footbridge at Shipley. 308 143 calls at the renumbered platform 2 on a Leeds to Skipton working in February 2001. *(Martin Bairstow)*

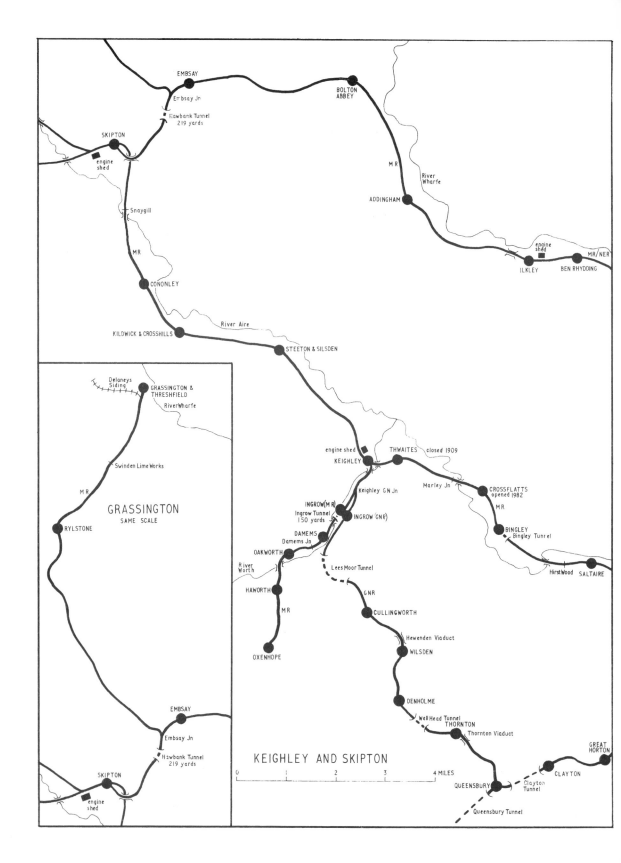

EMBSAY

BOLTON ABBEY

Embsay Jn

Hawbank Tunnel
219 yards

SKIPTON

engine
shed

MR

River
Wharfe

ADDINGHAM

Snaygill

MR

engine
shed

ILKLEY

MR/NER

BEN RHYDDING

CONONLEY

River Aire

KILDWICK & CROSSHILLS

STEETON & SILSDEN

Delaneys
Siding

GRASSINGTON &
THRESHFIELD

RiverWharfe

Swinden LimeWorks

MR

GRASSINGTON

SAME SCALE

RYLSTONE

engine shed

THWAITES   closed 1909

KEIGHLEY

Keighley GN Jn

Marley Jn

CROSSFLATTS
opened 1982

INGROW(MR)

Ingrow Tunnel
150 yards

INGROW (GNR)

MR

BINGLEY

Bingley Tunnel

DAMEMS

Damems Jn

OAKWORTH

River
Worth

Lees Moor Tunnel

HirstWood   SALTAIRE

HAWORTH

MR

GNR

CULLINGWORTH

Hewenden Viaduct

WILSDEN

OXENHOPE

DENHOLME

EMBSAY

Well Head Tunnel

THORNTON

Thornton Viaduct

GREAT
HORTON

Embsay Jn

Hawbank Tunnel
219 yards

KEIGHLEY AND SKIPTON

0   1   2   3   4 MILES

CLAYTON

SKIPTON

engine
shed

QUEENSBURY

Clayton
Tunnel

Queensbury Tunnel

Class 308 EMUs began to appear, in and amongst the diesels, during 1995, culminating in the new timetable, which began on 30 September. Leeds - Skipton and Leeds - Ilkley already were half hourly. Bradford - Ilkley and Bradford - Skipton were doubled to half hourly and a new half hourly service was introduced between Leeds and Bradford Forster Square. At the same time, four Leeds - Morecambe trains joined those from Leeds to Carlisle in running semi fast as far as Skipton, over and above the locals. These changes trebled the service out of Bradford Forster Square and gave Shipley 16 electric departures each hour plus the diesels on the Morecambe and Carlisle routes.

What didn't emerge was the enhanced through London service. The present, Summer 2002, timetable shows just two departures from Bradford Forster Square at 6.32am and 7.13pm on Mondays to Fridays. There is also a 6.40am from Skipton serving Keighley and Shipley. This is a diesel, with a class 43 at each end. Until a substation is provided at Skipton, a class 91 locomotive cannot draw power between Shipley and Skipton without risking stopping the other electric trains.

The reality is that GNER, the Inter City operator, will not run high speed trains off the high speed route, except for this tiny number of early morning and evening extensions. The Leeds - Kings Cross service is well on the way to achieving a half hourly frequency throughout the day. Stations in Airedale and Wharfedale have connections into virtually all

these trains. Bradford Council still thinks that trade in the City suffers from the lack of a more comprehensive through service.

As for through trains to the Continent, these have not materialised at all. The "North of London" rolling stock was built but the service was still born, a victim of budget airlines and red tape over Customs and Immigration. Rail travel to the Continent will become much easier when Eurostar services begin at Kings Cross rather than just Waterloo. But there are no plans for through trains from Bradford, nor anywhere else north of London.

The class 308s served until 1991. They were never trouble free and there were periods when the service was severely disrupted either for lack of rolling stock or shortage of drivers. There were nearly always odd diesel units covering one or two of the diagrams.

The operation was privatised, in 1997, but still largely governed by the PTE. In the short time since then, it has been known variously as Regional Railways North East, Northern Spirit and Arriva Trains Northern.

A condition of the franchise was the procurement of a fleet of new electric units. During 2001, 16 three car sets emerged. Designated class 333, they are based on the 332s on Heathrow Express. They were built at Zaragoza, in Spain from where they had to be transported by road to Hendaye on the French border because of the different gauge. They were put on the rails at

A class 43 diesel leads a Bradford Forster Square to Kings Cross High Speed Train into Shipley on 21 August 1998. The viewpoint is almost the same as the battered photo on page 37.

(Martin Bairstow)

Hendaye and hauled via the Channel Tunnel to Leeds. They are vastly superior to what passed before. The automatic public address announcements must drive regular users insane. On one occasion, I was advised seven times, between Shipley and Leeds that the next station was Leeds where the train would terminate and I should take my belongings with me. Other times I've been told, approaching Ben Rhydding, that the next stop was Bingley.

During 2002, eight of the 16 strong fleet acquired a fourth carriage. The remainder are to follow soon.

Communities left out

Between Bradford and Skipton, most of the closed stations have reopened. By contrast, between Leeds and Shipley, all the 1965 closures remain unavenged. This may be good if you are travelling through. In the evening peak, a commuter can easily be in Keighley when a car driver would still be held up on Kirkstall Road. The fast run from Leeds to Shipley, 11 miles in 12 minutes, has contributed much to the growth of traffic further into Airedale. Likewise, the non stop run from Leeds to Guiseley. One would wish to be very careful before compromising this position. I remember, some 40 years ago on a Leeds - Bradford local, a woman complaining "I've never known a train stop at so many stations" - and we'd only reached Newlay & Horsforth.

But look at the potential at some of the five demolished stations on this section. Apperley Bridge is on the main road between Harrogate and Bradford. Nearby Rawdon is on the road from Ilkley to Leeds, which merges at Kirkstall with the route from Shipley. Nobody from Rawdon is going to set off in the wrong direction to park a car at Guiseley Station, then travel into Leeds. They pay the same taxes to subsidise the train service but are disenfranchised from using it, just because four decades ago, Dr Beeching decided to close these five stations as part of a philosophy, which has no relevance today.

Calverley & Rodley is in a parallel position, just off the Leeds Ring Road. A new station would want to be on the Leeds side of the Ring Road and would require major road works or nobody could get into it.

In 1999, the PTE published its priority for new stations, identifying five in West Yorkshire, which should go ahead as soon as possible. They discarded Calverley & Rodley because Leeds Council had no enthusiasm for the attendant road works. They prioritised Apperley Bridge and Kirkstall. After four years, no progress has been made. Apperley Bridge would be closer to Shipley than before, accessed by the road leading to Esholt Sewerage Works, just across the road from the old station. It would, according to the PTE, be a major "park & ride" for North Bradford.

Besides cost, these two station proposals have other obstacles to overcome. Network Rail and Arriva Trains seem to think that the additional stops will wreck the timetable. Also, it is claimed that there is no room on the trains for any more passengers. At least that implies an acceptance that the facilities would generate traffic.

Has nobody noticed that the half hourly Leeds - Bradford Forster Square trains have plenty of spare capacity? Ever since their introduction in 1995, loadings have been a disappointment. They never will realise their potential until they are able to pick up traffic in the Aire Valley.

Site for a park & ride station? Just east of the Leeds Ring Road, near Calverley & Rodley, a class 110 "Calder Valley" set speeds towards Leeds on 9 April 1989. *(Martin Bairstow)*

Frizinghall Revisited – A Schoolboy Vindicated

This piece was written shortly after September 1987.

Monday 16 September 1963 marked a new chapter in my life as, sporting my cap and brown blazer, I entered the imposing and daunting edifice of Bradford Grammar School.

My seven year career was undistinguished. The only time I shone was in February 1969, after I had criticised the choice of visiting speakers who came weekly to address the sixth form. The master in charge asked if I could suggest anyone better. I said yes, so he advertised me as visiting speaker. For 40 minutes, I addressed an audience of over 150 on how the Government had carved up the British Railway Industry. Fortunately, no transcript was retained. I don't think it was too good, technically, but the consensus seemed to be that, at least, I had the courage of my convictions.

Before any of this could happen, I had to reach the place. Most pupils came by bus, though there was some rail traffic, mainly from Ilkley and Skipton directions. Because of the return train times, these pupils had to be issued with "early passes" by Mr J Breeze Bentley, a senior member of staff who was reputed to know *Bradshaw* by heart.

We lived in Greengates and my parents directed that I should go by bus. This involved a change in Bradford, the journey thence to school being on a trolley bus, destined to cease on the Manningham Lane route in November 1963.

To reach school for 8.50am, I had to set out from home at 7.50. I reasoned that I could leave at 8.10 and catch the 8.25 train from Apperley Bridge, which only took nine minutes to Frizinghall, giving plenty of time to walk up to school.

My Father said the City Council, which was responsible for my travel costs, would only pay bus not train fares. I responded that the train cost 7d per day against a shilling on the bus. My Father played his trump card - apparently "normal" people went by bus.

In those days, Bradford Grammar School functioned all day Mondays, Wednesdays and Fridays but mornings only Tuesdays, Thursdays and Saturdays. There was sporting activity on some half days but on others we were dismissed at 12.25pm.

My Mother quickly tired of me turning up wanting dinner at nearly two o'clock. The 12.41 train from Frizinghall would have me at Apperley Bridge at 12.50 and home just after 1pm, so it was decreed that on Saturday 28 September, I would go by train "as an experiment", which in the event lasted 18 months.

No sooner was one hurdle overcome than another appeared - the closure notice. This appeared in October 1963 covering local trains in Airedale and all services in Wharfedale. A total of 22 stations were threatened.

Opposition to closure was well orchestrated in Ilkley but elsewhere it was pathetic. I composed my

MIDLAND RAILWAY.

OPENING

OF NEW STATION AT

FRIZINGHALL

ON THE

LEEDS & BRADFORD BRANCH.

A STATION will be OPENED at FRIZINGHALL, between MANNINGHAM and SHIPLEY,

On MONDAY, FEB. 1st,

And from that date until further notice, Trains will call there as under:—

* Passengers travelling by these Trains to or from Leeds or intermediate Stations between Leeds and Shipley change Carriages at Shipley.

For times at intermediate Stations between Bradford and Skipton, and Bradford and Leeds see the published Time-Tables of the Company.

JAMES ALLPORT, General-Manager.

Derby, Jan. 26th, 1875.

Bemrose & Sons, Printers, London and Derby.

To celebrate the 1987 reopening, the Keighley & Worth Valley Railway unearthed this announcement of the first opening and published it as a post card.

own objection to the Transport Users Consulatative Committee and thus received the reams of paper, which are circulated to "official objectors". This revealed just how few people had actually bothered to put pen to paper. It also conveyed the depressing negative attitude of BR to everything. As many of the threatened stations would still have trains passing through, the question was inevitably raised why couldn't some of them be retained as unstaffed halts. The answer was that mothers would wheel prams over the barrow crossings between platforms and get killed.

Public hearings were held over two days at Ilkley in May 1964. In September, it was announced that 17 of the stations would close. Some people, including a lot of railway staff, believed there was still hope if Labour won the General Election on 15 October. They did, but there was no change of policy, despite Harold Wilson having made certain pledges during the campaign.

I last travelled to school by rail on a rather snowy Saturday 20 March 1965. As usual, I spent the afternoon and evening on the station at Apperley Bridge before taking a final trip to Calverley & Rodley and back.

The road level building at Frizinghall was demolished in the 1950s and the ticket office transferred to a waiting room on the right hand platform. View towards Bradford. *(D Thompson)*

"Next stop Frizinghall". Inside a brand new class 333 EMU, February 2001. *(Martin Bairstow)*

Mr J Breeze Bentley had not yet given up. He posted a notice at school, claiming that it might just be possible to persuade the Minister to retain Frizinghall, as an unstaffed halt if parents would fill in a form detailing the hardship, which their offsprings were now suffering. Mine refused on the grounds that my travelling arrangements had merely returned to "normal". So I did it myself.

I travelled by bus for two years. Then, from the Spring of 1967, I cycled. Every day I pedalled up Frizinghall Road, noting that the station remained in situ long after the others had been demolished. It was not until early 1972 that the bulldozers moved in.

Later that year, Bradford Council offered a rescue package to save the remaining trains from Forster Square to Ilkley and Keighley. A more enlightened BR then accepted the offer from Baildon Council to finance rehabilitation of the station there. The cost was modest because the platforms were still in place. If only those at Frizinghall had remained another year, reopening would quite likely have followed in the mid 1970s. Promises to reopen Frizinghall and Steeton & Silsden actually came up at the 1973 local elections, the first ones for the wider Bradford authority and for the PTE.

The 1975/6 timetable allowed extra time for trains to stop at Frizinghall, but BR said the PTE offer was insufficient to cover the cost of rebuilding the platforms. The scheme had to wait another 12 years.

In 1981, the PTE announced a three year plan to build nine unstaffed halts, mostly on the sites of abandoned stations. By 1984, they had achieved six

including Saltaire, but then there was a pause whilst they blamed the forthcoming abolition of the Metropolitan County Council for lack of further progress.

Once that was out of the way, the reconstituted PTE gave the go ahead, in April 1986, for two further stations, one of which was Frizinghall. So, finally on 7 September 1987, Frizinghall came back to life - in time for the new school term but 17 years too late for me. None - the - less, I managed a trip to Guiseley and back during the first week.

I boarded at the up platform, which is on the same spot from which I had last departed 22½ years earlier. The scene had changed somewhat in the intervening time. Gone were the goods lines, the yard the semaphores and the signal box, now on the Worth Valley of course. No longer could one see the platforms at Manningham Station, nor the intermediate box at Manningham Sidings. More important, where was the coal fired waiting room where I sometimes did my homework?

I remembered the teacher who used to threaten his less industrious students: *You'll come to a sticky end. You'll end up selling tickets at Frizinghall Station.*

More seriously, I recalled the paltry bit of public money they were going to save by closing Frizinghall Station. This I compared with the cost of putting it back again.

The 12 year old schoolboy, now 35, felt vindicated.

308143, on a Bradford F S to Leeds working, calls at Frizinghall in1996, after the up platform had been widened to accommodate traffic from Bradford Grammar School.   (Stuart Baker)

Lineside Logs

Thanks to David Holmes, we can catch a glimpse of traffic passing through Calverley & Rodley during a two hour period on the evening of Friday 31 July 1959. We start off with the only named train of the evening and the only one double headed, as "Black Five" No 44756 and Ivatt "Mogull" No 43030 come through on the "Devonian" from Paignton to Bradford Forster Square. A minute later, we have the "Derby Slow" stopping at platform 2. Comprising more parcels vans than passenger stock, this was the only steam train still booked to call at Calverley & Rodley.

Moving on to Armley Canal Road, David's log covers just over two hours on a Saturday afternoon, 5 December 1959. The period includes passage in both directions of the two named Anglo - Scottish expresses. The "Waverley" ran from London St Pancras to Edinburgh, the "Thames - Clyde" to Glasgow St Enoch. The northbound workings are in the hands of consecutively numbered "Royal Scot" class 4-6-0s, 46112 "Sherwood Forester" and 46113 "Cameronian". The corresponding southbound trains were headed by "Britannia" class 4-6-2s, then only a few years old: 70044 "Earl Haig" and 70053 "Moray Firth".

Time	Line	Loco	Working	
6.28pm	Down Slow	DMU	Leeds - Bradford	Stopping
6.31pm	Down Fast		"44756 + 43030 "Devonian"	
6.32pm	Up Fast	46493	Bradford - Derby slow	Stopping
6.33pm	Down Slow	DMU	Leeds - Ilkley	Stopping
6.36pm	Down Slow	48157	Empty stock	
6.42pm	Up Slow	43018	Morecambe - Leeds	
6.54pm	Down Slow	48311	Freight	
6.55pm	Up Slow	DMU	Bradford - Leeds	Stopping
6.55pm	Down Fast	42139	Scarborough - Bradford	
7.00pm	Up Slow	92155	Freight	
7.02pm	Down Fast	DMU	Leeds - Bradford	Stopping
7.04pm	Up Slow	92082	Freight	
7.05pm	Up Fast	43999	Freight	
7.06pm	Down Slow	43039	Freight	
7.10pm	Down Fast	43112	St Pancras - Bradford	
7.25pm	Down Fast	44007	Freight	
7.27pm	Up Slow	43043	Carnforth - Leeds	
7.30pm	Up Fast	44943	Freight	
7.31pm	Down Slow	DMU	Leeds - Ilkley	Stopping
7.34pm	Up Slow	40193	Parcels	
7.36pm	Down Slow	73156	Leeds - Heysham extra	
7.39pm	Up Slow	92167	Freight	
7.49pm	Up Slow	43960	Freight	
7.54pm	Up Fast	DMU	Bradford - Leeds	Stopping
8.00pm	Down Fast	DMU	Leeds - Bradford	Stopping
8.16pm	Up Slow	44577	Freight	
8.22pm	Up Slow	DMU	Ilkley - Leeds	Stopping

Time	Line	Loco	Working	
1.50pm	Down Fast	DMU	Leeds - Bradford	Stopping
1.50pm	Up Slow	90136	Freight	
1.57pm	Down Fast	42139	Bristol - Bradford	
2.02pm	Down Slow	46113	"Waverley"	
2.04pm	Up Slow	48443	Empty vans	
2.05pm	Up Fast	DMU	Bradford - Leeds	Stopping
2.06pm	Down Slow	43052	Leeds - Morecambe	
2.20pm	Up Slow	70053	"Thames - Clyde"	
2.21pm	Down Slow	DMU	Leeds - Ilkley	Stopping
2.33pm	Up Fast	DMU	Ilkley - Leeds	Stopping
2.50pm	DownFast	DMU	Leeds - Bradford	Stopping
2.52pm	Up Slow	44467	Freight	
2.59pm	Up Slow	45364	Morecambe - Leeds	
3.05pm	Up Fast	DMU	Bradford - Leeds	Stopping
3.13pm	Down Fast	42928	Parcels	
3.13pm	Down Slow	46112	"Thames - Clyde"	
3.22pm	Down Fast	DMU	Leeds - Ilkley	Stopping
3.31pm	Down Slow	44966	Leeds - Morecambe	
3.33pm	Up Fast	DMU	Ilkley - Leeds	Stopping
3.39pm	Down Fast	44672	Freight	
3.40pm	Up Slow	70044	"Waverley"	
3.41pm	Down Slow	42132 + 42900	Light engines	
3.48pm	Up Slow	48283	Freight	
3.50pm	Down Fast	DMU	Leeds - Bradford	Stopping
3.54pm	Down Slow	48652	Freight	
3.58pm	Down Slow	42052	Light engine	

"Britannia" class No 70053 "Moray Firth" was a regular performer on the "Thames Clyde Express". It is seen approaching Calverley & Rodley on 26 June 1960.

(P B Booth/ N E Stead collection)

LMS 3 cylinder compound No 41071 entering Calverley & Rodley with a local, probably for Ilkley, as a train from Bradford restarts for Leeds on 27 May 1957. The compound was withdrawn later that year.

(J C W Halliday)

"Jubilee" class No 45573 "Newfoundland" passing Armley Canal Road on the "down slow" with a freight from Hunslet to Carlisle on 10 March 1964.

(David Holmes)

Round The Corner

Signalman at Shipley Goods
by Richard D Pulleyn

The Shipley signalmen were a very special team. I first got to know them in the late 1960's - steam had only just disappeared from the scene, but the spirit lived on with a shunting loco used by Crossley's scrap merchants in their yard, an occasional enthusiasts' special trains, and the embryonic Keighley & Worth Valley Railway who would send their locos for turning "on the angle" - a local term which referred to the triangular layout at Shipley.

"Round the corner" was local term too - referring to the long curve running from Bradford Junction, at the southern apex of the triangle, to Shipley Goods signal box at the Bradford end of the goods yard.

At this time, Shipley Town Yard - so named to distinguish it from the former GNR yard at Shipley Windhill - still saw a respectable amount of traffic. A firm of importers, who received "ferry wagons" from the continent, used the former wool warehouse and goods shed. The adjacent sidings, north of Valley Road overbridge, were used by Crossley's as a small scrap yard, and the coal yard south of the bridge was still used by a number of merchants for its original purpose.

By then, Shipley Goods was only open for one shift each day - from 7.45 a.m. to 4.45 p.m., Monday to Friday - "Office hours!" was the joke among other signalmen who were used to working a three shift pattern which still applied at most boxes - 6.00 a.m. to 2.00 p.m. was "Days", 2.00 p.m. to 10.00 p.m. was "Lates", and 10.00 p.m. to 6.00 a.m., of course, was "Nights".

Gerry Harding had transferred from the three shift 'box at Shipley Bingley Junction to be on "Permanent Days" as regular signalman at Shipley Goods. He had a young family and supplemented his income by running a milk round before his signalling duties, then collecting insurance premiums in the evenings - a real hard worker, holding down three jobs. One morning an engine was on its way from Bradford Valley Yard to pick up

traffic from Shipley Goods yard; the Up Home signal at Shipley Goods remained stubbornly in the "on" position, so the driver sounded his horn but nothing happened. The guard walked up to the signal box and found Gerry lifeless on the floor; an ambulance was summoned but he never recovered. I'm not sure about the medical cause of his death, maybe it was sheer exhaustion, but he was still a relatively young man. The camaraderie and fellowship among the Shipley signalmen at that time was such that they worked together to help Gerry's widow and children; Mr Munton, the Assistant Area Manager and former Station Master at Shipley, coordinated efforts.

Relief Signalmen temporarily covered the vacancy created by Gerry's untimely death, but the shift arrangement was not popular because it didn't fit easily with the normal pattern. The men knew about my interest in railway signalling, so they encouraged me to speak to the District Signalmen's Inspector, Mr Jack Newman, about applying for the vacancy. Shortly afterwards, having been well tutored by a number of experienced signalmen, I passed the "Rules and Regulations" examination and was appointed to train for the job.

Given my previous experience as a Relief Train Recorder and Crossing Keeper, it didn't take long for me to learn the traffic; by the end of the week, the relief signalman who was training me was needed on other duties, so I was examined "in post" and "passed out" for my first signalman's position.

I still have a couple of train registers from Shipley Goods at that time and, looking back, it quite surprises me how much traffic there was; on each shift we would fill a complete page for about 40 signalled moves in each direction. Although the name of the signal box was Shipley Goods, it should be made clear that during the shift we signalled all trains between Shipley and Bradford Forster Square and Shipley. The Goods lines were closed in 1970, but two lines were adequate for the remaining traffic. The regular passenger services were from Bradford Forster Square to Ilkley ("Up the Branch")

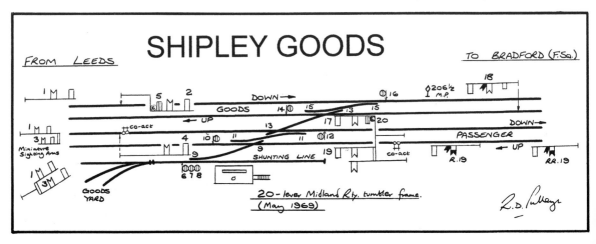

SHIPLEY 1910

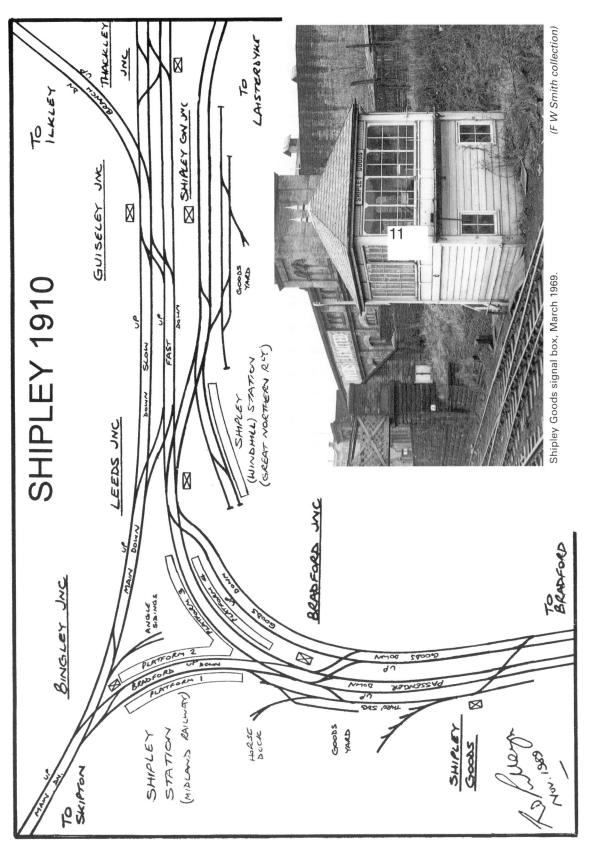

TO ILKLEY

BRADFORD JNC
THACKLEY JNC

GUISELEY JNC

SHIPLEY GN JNC

TO LAISTERDYKE

LEEDS JNC

UP DOWN SLOW
UP FAST
DOWN

GOODS YARD

SHIPLEY (WINDHILL) STATION (GREAT NORTHERN RLY.)

BINGLEY JNC

MAIN UP DOWN

ANGLE SIDINGS

PLATFORM 3

PLATFORM DOWN

GOODS UP

BRADFORD JNC

PLATFORM 2

BRADFORD UP DOWN

PLATFORM 1

GOODS DOWN

UP

PASSENGER DOWN

UP

THRO' SDG.

SHIPLEY GOODS

TO BRADFORD

MAIN UP DN.

TO SKIPTON

SHIPLEY STATION (MIDLAND RAILWAY)

HORSE DOCK

GOODS YARD

R J [signature] Nov. 1989

Shipley Goods signal box, March 1969.

(F W Smith collection)

SHIPLEY GOODS

11

69

and to Keighley; connections could be made at Shipley or Keighley into trains from Leeds to Skipton, Morecambe and Carlisle. Parcels trains provided important revenue from Forster Square - mostly mail order goods from Grattan's in Bradford.

The real interest at Shipley Goods, however, was provided by the "Trip" workings; these were local freight trains, mostly operating from Bradford Valley Yard to Shipley, Ilkley and Keighley; up to six trains worked into and out of Shipley Yard each day. We also had a couple of regular "Engine and Van" workings out to Apperley Junction and Esholt Junction signal boxes to deliver water cans to the signalmen at those locations because they still had no running water.

At Shipley Goods signal box, we had the luxury of an outside water tap at the bottom of the steps; this was popular with the local allotment holders as well as the signalmen, and in return for its use we got an occasional lettuce or bag of tomatoes.

Lighting was still by gas lamps; they were fitted with fragile mantles that had to be treated very carefully otherwise they crumbled to dust. Cooking was also by gas, although we only had one ring so we were fairly limited in what we could prepare - I recall that eggs boiled in the kettle were quite popular because the "lever collar" (a safety device placed on levers to remind signalmen about the presence of a train) could be used as a make-shift egg cup. If we needed anything more substantial, Fearnley's Mill and Dye Works was behind the signal box and they had a canteen. Heating was provided

by a "Romesse" stove, fuelled by coke from a bunker outside the box; it was good practice to keep a couple of buckets of coke dry inside, together with any pieces of coal which had fallen from wagons during shunting; old sleepers were provided to chop for firewood. The toilet facilities were also rather primitive: known as an "Elson", this was simply a bucket, filled with a noxious chemical, and seat, that was housed in a little hut at the bottom of the signal box steps; the contents had to be emptied into a cess pit - not an attractive prospect, so we were paid one hour's overtime each week for "toilet duties"!

The Midland Railway had opened the signal box on 9 August 1903 to replace a previous structure; its proper title in official documents was "Shipley Goods Sidings", but the suffix was rarely used elsewhere. It had a 20 lever frame, with the old "Tumbler" locking still in place, right up to closure on Sunday 3 September 1972. After that date, all traffic to and from the yard had to be handled from the Bradford Junction end.

Today, Crossley's scrap metal business occupies the whole of the former goods yard, which is still served by an occasional train. The route has been electrified and the passenger service between Leeds and Bradford Forster Square has been restored; the train frequency is far more intensive than ever. Control of the signalling at Shipley was transferred to Leeds in July 1994 and since 2001 has been worked from the Control Centre (IECC) some 30 miles away at York.

"Jubilee" 4 - 6 - 0 No 45675 "Hardy" passing Shipley Goods on the "up goods" line with an evening Bradford to Carlisle freight on 19 June 1967. The goods lines from Manningham were opened in 1876 but closed in 1970.   (G W Morrison)

The Worth Valley Branch

Since the Worth Valley Railway was opened, it has been the means already of bringing thousands of visitors to the ancient village of Haworth. During the past few Sundays, hundreds have been seen enjoying the pure air and mountain breezes in the romantic neighbourhood. To all appearances it is very likely to become a general pleasure locality in the summer months.

—Keighley News 25 May 1867.

Three and a half miles to the south of Keighley, Haworth is known for its association with the Brontes. Members of the family invested in early railways and Branwell Bronte secured employment for a short time on the Manchester & Leeds, until he was sacked for being drunk. Although, none of the Brontes lived long enough to see the railway reach Haworth, they have posthumously helped sustain the level of passenger traffic on the Worth Valley branch by keeping up the numbers of tourists.

The 1845 Act for the Leeds & Bradford Extension Railway included a branch to Haworth. It may have been wishful thinking, even a ploy to "buy" support of influential people in the Worth Valley for the Company's main line. The branch idea died in the post "Railway Mania" recession of the late 1840s.

The peak of the "Railway Mania" had been reached in October 1845. That month saw advertisements for a proposed Manchester, Hebden Bridge & Keighley Junction Railway, which would have linked the Manchester & Leeds at Hebden Bridge with the Leeds & Bradford at Keighley. The route would have been 12 miles in length with a long tunnel under Oxenhope Moor. Nothing came of it.

October 1861 brought a deputation of local businessmen to the Midland Railway headquaters at Derby. Agreement was reached that a local Company would build a branch line from Keighley to Oxenhope. The Midland would work it upon completion. The track was to be single but sufficient land purchased to allow doubling at a later date.

The Act was passed in June 1862 but work did not begin until February 1864. Progress was frustrated by subsidence in the 150 yard Ingrow tunnel. A newly built Methodist Church above collapsed and the Railway had to pay compensation. On I November 1866, the Contractor was able to run a train over the entire line but hopes of an early opening date were dashed by the floods of 14 November, the same incident which caused Apperley Viaduct to collapse. Forty yards of track were washed away near Damems, leaving the track suspended over the gap. This, and minor damage elsewhere, delayed the opening until Saturday 13 April 1867.

The opening day was wet and the inaugural train failed to get to grips with the 1 in 58 out of Keighley. It succeeded at the second attempt, only to stall between Oakworth and Haworth. It had to be divided to complete the journey to Oxenhope.

The large Goods Yard at Haworth has become the base for the Preservation Society's fleet of steam and diesel power. Here it is seen in its authentic role, being shunted by 3F 0 - 6 - 0 No 43586, the last engine to work the branch under British Railways. *(Peter Sunderland)*

Carrying the 20F Skipton shed plate, Midland 3F 0 - 6 - 0 No 43784 emerges from Ingrow Tunnel with a train for Oxenhope about 1950. Hidden behind the train is the ground frame for the private siding into Clough`s Mill on the left.
(D Ibbotson)

The Midland Takeover and New Works

The working arrangement with the Midland Railway lasted until 1 July 1881, when the main line Company gained ownership of the branch. They had to do this because expenditure was required at Keighley in anticipation of the arrival of the Great Northern Railway from Bradford Exchange and Halifax. Opened in 1884, this emerged from Lees Moor Tunnel and entered the Worth Valley at a point overlooking Damems. It then descended through its own station at Ingrow, adjacent to that on the Worth Valley branch which it came alongside at GN Junction, 3/4 mile outside Keighley. Here there was a connection allowing Great Northern passenger trains to join the Worth Valley line which was doubled into Keighley, where a new station had opened on 6 May 1883. Great Northern goods traffic continued parallel to the Worth Valley line until it crossed under to reach its own goods yard. The new Keighley Station was positioned on the junction with two platforms, plus a bay on the main line and two at an angle for Worth Valley and Great Northern traffic. The route out of Keighley Station was not just doubled but substantially rebuilt with a stone supported embankment in place of the original 13 arch viaduct.

Three signal boxes were provided at GN Junction. The Midland had one controlling its end of the connection onto the Great Northern, which had its own box in the reciprocal position. Then the Midland had another one at the point where the Worth Valley branch reduced to single track. From here to Oxenhope, the branch was worked as one "staff and ticket" section. From 4 April 1900, line capacity was increased with the commissioning of passing loops and signal boxes at Oakworth and Haworth. Electric token working was introduced, except on the final section to Oxenhope, which retained a staff. The passing loops could not cross two passenger trains.

On Sunday 6 November 1892, the line was diverted for nearly half a mile south of Oakworth in order to bypass the timber trestle viaduct over the Vale Mill Dam. The new route involved a three arch viaduct, four other bridges and the short Mytholmes Tunnel, all built substantially in stone, wide enough for double track which was never needed.

In 1924, the layout at GN Junction was simplified and placed under the control of one Midland signal box. The layout was shortened by singling the connection between the two railways but imposing a harsher gradient.

Passenger Service

Bradshaw for October 1867 shows six trains from Oxenhope to Keighley on weekdays and four on Sundays All stop at every station apart from Damems, which has only two weekday calls. The first departure was not until 8.00am so they were not, at that stage, catering for early morning workmen .Indeed some of the trains were first and second class only - no third. By 1880, the service had risen to eight trains on weekdays, including early morning provision, and five on Sundays. By this time, all trains on the Midland Railway conveyed first and third class carriages. Second class had been abolished on 1 January1875 and the standard of third class had been brought up to that of the previous second. The station master at Oxenhope was sent a supply of "third" labels with which to redesignate the second class compartments on the branch train pending eventual repainting.

From 1883, workmen were entitled by statute to travel at reduced fares provided that their outward journey was completed before 8.00. In 1902, a Board of Trade inspector conducted an enquiry into an alleged failure by the Midland Railway to provide adequate facilities for workmen in the Keighley area under the 1883 Act. By this time there were about 16 trains each weekday beginning with a 5.12 from

An Oxenhope to Keighley DMU passing the closed station at Damems in August 1960. The hut on the platform is for the relief crossing keeper who would not have access to the house, from which the resident keeper operated.

(Martin Bairstow collection)

Oakworth Station and signal box looking towards Keighley in 1955, shortly before the passing loop was removed.

(Peter Sunderland)

44055 passing the recently closed station at Ingrow with the Worth Valley pick up goods early in 1962. The main building at Ingrow was not in similar style to other branch stations until the Preservation Society imported the present structure from Foulridge in the late 1980s. *(D J Mitchell)*

Oxenhope. People starting work in Keighley at 6am asked for that to run 15 minutes later but the Railway said it had to be back in Haworth with workers, who started at 6am there. Others wanted the 7.53am from Oxenhope to start earlier so as to reach Keighley in time to qualify for workmen's tickets. The Board of Trade adjudicated in favour of the Railway who couldn't make their timetable please everybody. But it must have been hard on people who worked long hours with no flexi time if the trains didn't suit.

The branch service reached its maximum during the 1930s with 19 departures from Oxenhope, Mondays to Fridays, 21 Saturdays and six on Sundays. There were slightly fewer trains advertised the other way because some ran empty stock, passing the scheduled trains at Oakworth or Haworth. Push - pull operation allowed turn round times to be reduced to three minutes.

Decline and Closure

Cuts imposed during the Second World War were only partially restored afterwards. The Sunday service was withdrawn in 1947 and Damems closed in May 1949. Long gaps were left between trains during the middle of the day. Early in 1956, the signal boxes and passing loops were removed at Oakworth and Haworth leaving a "one engine in steam" section from GN Junction to Oxenhope. About the same time a three coach gangwayed push - pull set was introduced so that the guard could issue tickets. Oxenhope had become an unstaffed halt in 1955 and Ingrow followed three years later.

The guard used a setright machine, then popular on buses. He could issue tickets beyond Keighley but wasn't always keen to do so. When a Mrs Grey asked for a day return to Bingley, he protested that he would have to go back to his van to look up the fare. He issued the ticket but advised her next time to go by bus.

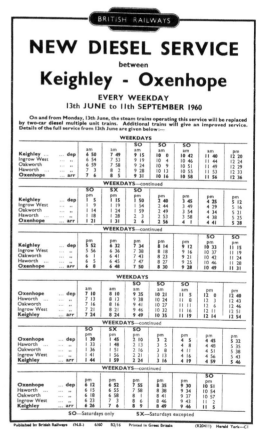

BRITISH RAILWAYS

NEW DIESEL SERVICE
between
Keighley - Oxenhope
EVERY WEEKDAY
13th JUNE to 11th SEPTEMBER 1960

On and from Monday, 13th June, the steam trains operating this service will be replaced by two-car diesel multiple unit trains. Additional trains will give an improved service. Details of the full service from 13th June are given below :—

WEEKDAYS

		am	am	SO am	SO am	SO am	am	pm
Keighley	dep	6 50	7 49	9 15	10 0	10 42	11 40	12 20
Ingrow West	,,	6 54	7 53	9 19	10 4	10 46	11 44	12 24
Oakworth	,,	6 59	7 58	9 24	10 9	10 51	11 49	12 29
Haworth	,,	7 3	8 2	9 28	10 13	10 55	11 53	12 33
Oxenhope	arr	7 6	8 5	9 31	10 16	10 58	11 56	12 36

WEEKDAYS—continued

		SO pm	SX pm	pm	pm	pm	pm	pm
Keighley	dep	1 5	1 15	1 50	2 40	3 45	4 25	5 12
Ingrow West	,,	1 9	1 19	1 54	2 44	3 49	4 29	5 16
Oakworth	,,	1 14	1 24	1 59	2 49	3 54	4 34	5 21
Haworth	,,	1 18	1 28	2 3	2 53	3 58	4 38	5 25
Oxenhope	arr	1 21	1 31	2 6	2 56	4 1	4 41	5 28

WEEKDAYS—continued

		pm	pm	pm	pm	pm	SO pm	SO pm
Keighley	dep	5 52	6 32	7 34	8 14	9 12	10 33	11 15
Ingrow West	,,	5 56	6 36	7 38	8 18	9 16	10 37	11 19
Oakworth	,,	6 1	6 41	7 43	8 23	9 21	10 42	11 24
Haworth	,,	6 5	6 45	7 47	8 27	9 25	10 46	11 28
Oxenhope	arr	6 8	6 48	7 50	8 30	9 28	10 49	11 31

WEEKDAYS

		am	am	am	SO am	SO am	pm	pm
Oxenhope	dep	7 10	8 10	9 35	10 21	11 5	12 0	12 40
Haworth	,,	7 13	8 13	9 38	10 24	11 8	12 3	12 43
Oakworth	,,	7 16	8 16	9 41	10 27	11 11	12 6	12 46
Ingrow West	,,	7 21	8 21	9 46	10 32	11 16	12 11	12 51
Keighley	arr	7 24	8 24	9 49	10 35	11 19	12 14	12 54

WEEKDAYS—continued

		SO pm	SX pm	SO pm	pm	pm	pm	pm
Oxenhope	dep	1 30	1 45	2 10	3 2	4 5	4 45	5 32
Haworth	,,	1 33	1 48	2 13	3 5	4 8	4 48	5 35
Oakworth	,,	1 36	1 51	2 16	3 8	4 11	4 51	5 38
Ingrow West	,,	1 41	1 56	2 21	3 13	4 16	4 56	5 43
Keighley	arr	1 44	1 59	2 24	3 16	4 19	4 59	5 46

WEEKDAYS—continued

		pm	pm	pm	pm	pm	SO pm	
Oxenhope	dep	6 12	6 52	7 55	8 35	9 30	10 51	
Haworth	,,	6 15	6 55	7 58	8 38	9 34	10 54	
Oakworth	,,	6 18	6 58	8 1	8 41	9 37	10 57	
Ingrow West	,,	6 23	7 3	8 6	8 46	9 43	11 2	
Keighley	arr	6 26	7 6	8 9	8 49	9 46	11 5	

SO—Saturdays only   SX—Saturdays excepted

Published by British Railways (N.E.)   6/60   B2/16   Printed in Great Britain   (R20411)   Herald York—C1

In July 1959, BR issued a formal closure notice. Keighley Corporation mounted a coherent case against closure. Under the prevailing (pre 1962) legislation, closure had to be approved by the Transport Users Consultative Committee who, three times, postponed making a decision. On 13 June 1960, an improved service was introduced with

Haworth Box closed in 1956, when the branch from G N Junction to Oxenhope was reduced to a single "one engine in steam" section. In recent times, the former Esholt Junction Box has been re erected here but not yet commissioned.

(Peter Sunderland)

The periodic visit of the Inspection saloon is mentioned in Bill Smith`s text on page 92. On 13 May 1958, the York saloon was propelled along the Worth Valley branch by "Standard" 2 - 6 - 0 No 77012 from Whitby Shed.

(Peter Sunderland)

Three months later, the Leeds Inspection coach was seen in Haworth Station with Ivatt 2 - 6 - 0 No 46493.

(Mrs A Sunderland)

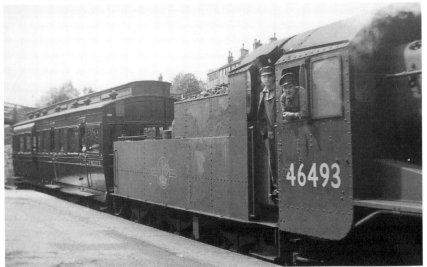

diesel multiple units replacing steam and filling in the previous gaps, except during the morning Monday to Friday when the pick up goods was about its business. The threat did not go away and passenger closure was approved for the end of 1961, with goods to follow six months later. The last train was a four car DMU at 11.15pm from Keighley. Normally it returned empty stock but, on this occasion, it was booked to stop at all stations on the return.

Revival

The concept of a volunteer supported railway had been pioneered by the Talyllyn in 1951. Ralph Povey, a resident of Oakworth had followed the fortunes of the early preservation schemes. In November 1961, he had a letter printed in the Bradford *Telegraph & Argus* suggesting that a preservation society be formed to take over the doomed Worth Valley branch. Meanwhile, Bob Cryer had also been writing to the local press. In 1960, his call had been for restoration of passenger service over the ex GN line from Keighley to Bradford. He got nowhere but the demise of the GN route persuaded him that the Worth Valley branch should not suffer the same fate.

On 24 January 1962, a public meeting was held in the Temperance Hall, Keighley. Attendance was encouraging and a committee was delegated to explore the possibilities. This reported back that some local businesses were in support, that BR had not rejected the idea out of hand and that a private loco owner had promised to make his engine available. A further meeting was called for 1 March at the Temperance Hall. At this, the Keighley & Worth Valley Railway Preservation Society was formed with Bob Cryer as its first Chairman and Ralph Povey on its governing body.

The first tangible sign of activity was the organising of a special train from Bradford Forster Square to Oxenhope on Saturday 23 June 1962. In those days, a special excursion was an easy thing to book. The local office for the purpose was at Bingley

Station. The incumbent there misunderstood totally the purpose of Bob Cryer's enquiry, advising him that his proposed trip might draw more support if it ran to Morecambe rather than Oxenhope. That hurdle overcome, the six coach special ran behind 3F No 43586, which had been a regular on the branch goods. The train was the last BR operation on the branch, which had closed to goods the previous week. After that, the track was no longer maintained. To emphasise the point, a single rail was removed at GN Junction where the box was closed leaving just a single track in use from Keighley Station to the goods yard at Ingrow (GN).

The Society tried to negotiate a lease with BR. This had happened with the Bluebell Railway in Sussex in 1960 but BR would have none of it, insisting on outright sale or nothing. Businesses who had expressed support were unwilling to help financially. Keighley Corporation, which had opposed closure of the line, wanted no part in its reopening. The break through came in September 1964 when BR agreed to sell the branch on deferred terms. Optimistically, the Society announced Whitsuntide 1965 as the reopening date. That target proved to be out by some three years and one month.

It took what seemed an eternity to achieve three vital stages in the transfer of ownership. First the exact boundary had to be agreed. No sooner was this done than BR decided to include in the sale the section between Keighley Station and GN Junction. This followed withdrawal, in June 1965, of the remaining goods traffic to Ingrow. Previously, it had been assumed that the Society would have to rent one track over this stretch with the other still used by BR. Then BR had to apply for an Order bringing the line within the jurisdiction of the Light Railways Act 1896. Finally, the powers under this Order had to be transferred to the Society's Operating Company under a second Light Railway Order.

On 29 June 1968, the "Reopening Special" finally set off behind 2-6-2T No 41241 and 0-6-0T No 30072.

From 1884 until 1965, the single line began at Keighley GN Junction, where a new signal box was provided in 1924, replacing the three boxes previously required. The signalman has just retrieved the token from the driver of an Oxenhope to Keighley push - pull in Summer 1955.

The bracket signal was retrieved by the Preservation Society and, with the addition of an arm for the loop, it now controls the Northbound approach to Damems Junction. *(Peter Sunderland)*

Haworth to Huddersfield

By Peter Sunderland

A push - pull set arriving at Keighley from Oxenhope, about 1952.   *(D Ibbotson)*

I started working at Milnsbridge, near Huddersfield in June 1953. Until the first winter, I travelled by motorcycle. The distance by road was 21½ miles and I could do the journey, if urgent, in 23 minutes in good conditions. This could involve 90 mph down Brighouse Hill, which now has houses on both sides and a 30mph limit. There was no overall 70 mph limit in those days. Derestricted meant just that.

There was little road traffic about, even in Brighouse and Huddersfield, but neither man nor machine could stand up to the pace, especially when the winter weather set in. Snow and frost brought realization that "digs" would be a better option for Mondays to Fridays.

So on Monday mornings I had to leave home at 6.05, down the fields to Haworth Station, where Raymond Newsholme already had a good fire going in the waiting room (the present day shop). He wasn't on the Railway staff but was there to collect newspapers off the first train up the Valley, the 6am from Keighley, due Haworth at 6.13. He set out a selection of papers for passengers to help themselves and leave the money while he carried the rest, in a sack, up the hill to his Father's shop in Haworth Village. The push - pull set had gone up to Oxenhope. I boarded it for Keighley at 6.22. At that period, it was still compartment stock, with an Ivatt 2-6-2T at the Oxenhope end.

From Keighley, the train service was more frequent to Bradford than to Leeds. Trains through from Skipton were supplemented by a few starting from the bay at the far end of platform one. The 6.51 had me in Forster Square with plenty of time to cross to Exchange Station. From there I had a choice of train for Huddersfield, the 7.40 via Halifax or 7.50 via Cleckheaton. Both took 49 minutes. From Huddersfield Station, I got a lift with the designer to reach work about 8.55.

I had to rebook for Huddersfield at Bradford Exchange. I always asked for a single until, one day the clerk gave me a day return. I queried it but he assured me that this was cheaper than a single. I was pleased but annoyed it had taken them so long to tell me.

The return on Friday involved different options. Until closure of the Queensbury Line in 1955, I tried to come back by that route. Bus to Huddersfield, 5.57 train to Halifax, 6.45 from there either to Ingrow or Cullingworth where my Father picked me up.

Halifax Station was a dismal dirty windy hole in which to wait for trains. The GN platform was uneven, the holes filled with water with a layer of oil on top. All the passenger trains had N1 tanks on. The carriages were old Howlden almost flat roof stock. They were rough riding wooden bodied bogie coaches. No toilets and usually no linoleum on the floor. If there was a light, it was electric but the gas fittings were still in place.

The big glass bowl, the outer shade of the gas lamp, still hung, filling very slowly with water from a leak in the roof. The dirty water swished round in the bowl as the train negotiated the curves and gradients. The compartment stank of stale gas and stagnant water. They seemed to keep the Howlden stock for the infrequent Halifax - Keighley trains. Bradford to Halifax and Keighley runs were usually with better appointed Gresley carriages.

Haworth to Huddersfield was always bound to be a difficult journey by rail, but has it got any worse over the past 50 years? Nowadays, Peter would need a bus at 6.07am from Haworth Station but this would pick up outside his house a few minutes earlier. That would compensate for the walk between bus and rail stations in Keighley. From there, he would have a GNER through London train at 6.50 getting him into Leeds for the 7.22 "Trans Pennine Express" to Huddersfield, arrive 7.43, a clear 45 minutes ahead of the 1953 schedule. He would get a carpet on the floor, a toilet, fluorescent lighting, no leaking roof and a free "Metro" newspaper. None of which can compete with the private car on a journey from Haworth to Huddersfield but the train has become a more realistic option for many commuter flows.

Ivatt 2 - 6 - 2T No 41326 calls at Haworth with a Keighley to Oxenhope push - pull on a Saturday in July 1955.
(Peter Sunderland)

In June 1960, to cover for a shortage of diesels, an additional push - pull set was put together using 41325 and an ex LNER non corridor driving trailer from Copley Hill. *(Peter Sunderland)*

A Promise Unfulfilled

The revived Worth Valley claims to be a "complete branch line" but has it lost its way?

The British Railways Board have now approved the sale of the branch to the Society and a limited company is being formed to complete negotiations. It is hoped that the Society will have a controlling interest in this company.

We aim to run a weekend tourist service (Haworth is already a world renowned tourist centre) starting during the summer of 1965, and soon after a daily commuter service, the exact time depending upon the completion of the legalities involved.

Volunteers will run the weekend services and maintain the railway until the commuter services are started when some permanent staff will be employed to assist voluntary workers. We expect that much traffic formerly lost to the railway will be restored and that there will be a good amount of interchange traffic between British Railways and ourselves. – Keighley & Worth Valley Railway *Prospectus* 1964

It was in response to this document that I joined the Society, aged 12, in 1964. Let me say at once that I owe a great deal to the Worth Valley Railway both in my career as a Chartered Accountant and in my interest as a Railway writer and publisher. I have nothing but admiration for the work put in by fellow members. Occasionally, it is a real pleasure to use the line in the normal course of business. One day in July 2002, I completed a VAT return for a client in Ilkley, caught the 11.22 electric train, changed at Shipley and Keighley and arrived for my next appointment in Haworth behind 2-6-2T No 41241.

Yet I list the Keighley & Worth Valley Railway as one of life's disappointments. The reason is to be found in the *Prospectus*, just quoted. The Organisation has never made the slightest attempt to achieve half of its declared main objective, the commuter service. It hasn't even exploited its tourist function to the full. The Railway is still closed on more days of the year than it is open. Traffic seems to be in long term decline. What has gone wrong?

Reopening Achieved

The hoped for 1965 date became 1966, then 1967 and finally 1968. By then, the line had not simply been closed for six years. It had crossed an epoch barrier. 1962 belonged to the pre Beeching era. Hence the infant Society thinking that it could retain the pick up goods and the early morning workmen. 1968 was another world. Car ownership had rocketed, not least amongst Society members, whilst branch line trains had all but disappeared elsewhere in the Country. If the latest Government "white paper" were to be believed, there would soon be no passenger trains on the main line through Keighley.

Unrealistic

I can remember, on a working party about 1965, a member arguing that we would have to keep the

The Railway offers concessions to residents but the train service is so limited.

train fare a penny less than the bus if we were to win back the traffic. Someone else thought that a tuppence differential might be necessary. Looking back, it all sounds so naïve and innocent. I can plead extreme youth but I was not alone in believing that railways could function without maintenance, that fuel was cheap and staff paid a pittance. The line had been closed as unprofitable because BR refused to acknowledge all revenue, whilst exaggerating costs.

We have to be grateful that there were some members around, with a measure of business experience, who embarked on a cautious approach, settling at first for an all volunteer weekend only operation. This quickly developed into something of a success, especially in 1971 when traffic doubled following release of *The Railway Children*. Operation was gradually extended to July and August weekdays and, by 1975, the Railway was claiming to carry as many passengers as it had in 1961, albeit of a rather different nature.

The Tourist Trade

The key to railway preservation has been the growth in leisure time. People rarely admit it, but most of us work shorter hours for a better standard of living than that achieved by our forebears. By the 1970s, this trend was well manifest in the numbers of people visiting Haworth and in the time which Worth

Re opening achieved. 41241 and 30072 double head out of Keighley on the first day, 29 June 1968.

(H Malham)

Amongst countless subsequent achievements has been the rebuilding, stone by stone at Ingrow, of the station from Foulridge on the Skipton to Colne line. The previous Ingrow building was destroyed during the period of closure.

(Martin Bairstow)

Another Worth Valley achievement was the return to traffic of Midland 4F No 43924, the first loco to be rescued from Barry Scrapyard. Arriving at Oxenhope on 1 March 1987. *(Tom Heavyside)*

people visiting Haworth and in the time which Worth Valley working members were able to devote to running the Railway.

We are now a whole generation further on from then. The trend has continued. There are even more tourists in the area, especially midweek and out of season. There also seem to be more working members on site. Yet, on the majority of days, there aren't any trains.

The pattern of service is roughly the same as it was in the mid 1970s but with patronage at least 25% lower. "Ordinary" traffic is down a great deal more than this but is made good in part by "Santa Specials" and "Thomas the Tank Engine" events. The Railway's core product, a trip behind steam has been diluted somewhat by Embsay & Bolton Abbey, Middleton, East Lancashire and countless others. Equally important, the pattern of family life has been altered out of recognition by such innovations as Sunday shopping and Sunday sport. There was a time when the Worth Valley Railway was one of the few outdoor leisure facilities open on a Sunday.

Tourism is now a seven days a week business. Yet the Railway has contracted the length of its midweek operating season. Having reached 14 consecutive weeks in 1994, it is now down to eight. The Railway seems to be chasing declining traffic by offering fewer trains on fewer days.

Some preserved railways have taken an opposite approach. In a competitive environment, they cannot rely on customers turning up only at the convenience of the working members. They cannot predict in advance which days will be disappointing because weather and other patterns may be different to last year. As like as not, if they try cutting out odd days, they'll end up scrapping the good ones. Better to advertise a daily service right through the Summer and kill any doubt as to whether the place is open to business or not. In 2003, the North Yorkshire Moors Railway operated every day from 29 March to 2 November. So, more or less, did Ravenglass & Eskdale, Ffestiniog, Talyllyn and Swanage with the Bluebell, Llangollen and Severn Valley not far behind.

Worth Valley apologists will say that these others "cheat" by employing paid operating staff but there was never anything in the *Prospectus* forbidding this and the Worth Valley does employ people in non operating positions.

Possibly the greatest difference between the Worth Valley and other major preserved lines is that the others have somebody in charge. The Worth Valley has always held the spectre of a General Manager to be the worst fate which could befall. Instead, it has management by committee, which seems to be a recipe for stagnation.

No matter how able and devoted the individuals, closet over 30 of them in a room, sometimes on licensed premises, for four hours till after 11pm on a midweek evening and it can bring out the worst. I

Some say that, without the democratic structure, the volunteers would not be motivated to work. Others are kept going by more basic considerations, such as the arrival of the tea trolley. Richard Pulleyn, Bruce Clarke and Len Smith partake, September 1996.

(F W Smith)

know from the years when I was Society Treasurer. I was as bad as anybody. I couldn't do it at all now. Drive home afterwards, then go to work the next day.

Ideas can be voted down, not on merit but on the identity of the individuals proposing them. It is called democracy but, in practice, it concentrates power on the few who can manage this lifestyle.

The Railway is not customer focussed. It is run by the working members for the working members, some of whom appear more interested in preserving the Railway exactly as it stands today, not as part of a national network - as was surely the original purpose. They even perceive further development of the Railway as a threat.

What Hope for Commuters?

If the Railway is too preoccupied to exploit the tourist market fully, then what chance the much more difficult task of mounting a daily service to carry people to their place of work?

Until 1995, the subject was never even considered. If it was mentioned, it was dismissed as impractical. Who was going to volunteer to drive a train or open a level crossing gate at 6am in all weather? Who was going to finance paid staff when no commuter railway in the World ran at a profit? Who was going to use it when car ownership was rising, buses frequent and neighbouring "main lines" under threat?

Who indeed? But that was the World of 1968, when Keighley looked set to lose its trains to Bradford and possibly Leeds as well.

35 years have elapsed since then. 2003 is at least as different from 1968 as that year was from 1962. Keighley has more than three times the number of passenger trains, carrying more people and serving a number of new and reopened intermediate stations. Saltaire and Steeton & Silsden had once

been considered as hopeless as Haworth and Oxenhope. Now they are an essential part of the transport system.

For how long can it be claimed that commuting from Steeton & Silsden makes sense but the thought of doing it from Haworth is still ridiculous? The present West Yorkshire PTE "Rail Plan" lists a feeder service from the Worth Valley as a longer term objective.

When the matter was first put before the Worth Valley committees in 1995, there was an uproar. The very notion was seen as a threat. Fears were fuelled by claims that the move could result in renationalisation and the imprisonment of working members for manslaughter. It was hard to believe that this was the same organisation, which had refused to take no for an answer in its formative years.

In 1995, there wasn't any PTE money actually on the table. Surely the response will have to be different if and when that stage comes. After all, existing Worth Valley business continues to decline and they are always pleading poverty, not least as the cost of maintaining steam locomotives rises relentlessly.

Practicalities

Distances in the Worth Valley are short. Buses are frequent. From Haworth to Keighley, there are four buses an hour in the daytime, two evenings and Sundays. From Oxenhope, there are two an hour, one evenings and Sundays. They are not unduly inhibited by traffic, but they do not serve the Railway Station in Keighley.

A Worth Valley rail service could only be justified as a feeder to the electric trains. It would have to be frequent and, above all, reliable.

PTE sponsored services run at least hourly, most of them better than that, from at least 7am until 11 at night. They run seven days a week, usually at half the weekday frequency on Sundays. To be consistent, a Worth Valley operation would need to be half hourly, day in day out. It would give tight connections into the Leeds trains but a wait for Bradford. Or maybe the other way round, depending on the majority traffic. The service would run Mondays to Fridays and would, presumably, be suspended during the daytime in mid Summer when steam would take over.

You couldn't have expensive 75 mph units doing a 9½ mile round trip every hour. We would have to be thinking of diesel stock, no longer in main line service. Such stock would need a proper budget for maintenance with undercover accommodation. The operation might be carried out by the Keighley & Worth Valley Railway or it could be contracted out. Either way, there would have to be tangible benefits to the KWVR. These might take the form of a flow of funds to underpin the preservation objective. For example, the existing "heritage" diesels might gain undercover accommodation with better equipment and working accommodation for those who strive to preserve them.

Its predecessor having abandoned the branch line for scrap, the PTE could not come along now and just trample on those who have preserved it. Neither could the preservationists declare that the Railway is private property, closed to those who would use it for public utility.

If the branch could provide a useful feeder to the electric service, then the PTE and KWVR would have to negotiate a deal which was fair to both parties There are many questions of detail such as gated level crossings, gas and paraffin lit stations and the interaction between two different operations on the same line. These are matters to discuss and resolve, they are not absolute barriers.

If there were found not to be sufficient demand for a commuter service, then the KWVR would continue providing a "heritage" operation, aimed mainly at the tourist market. There is a vague parallel with the Isle of Man, where buses provide the basic service with trains supplementing at times of tourists demand. Even that compromise requires the trains to run daily from May to October.

Turning Away Business

In September 1976, I worked for two weeks at a client in Oxenhope. Each lunchtime, I wandered down to the Station where I turned away potential customers with the news that the midweek train service had finished at the end of August. That year, the Railway had increased the period of daily operation from six to eight consecutive weeks. This had meant 40 midweek volunteer guard's turns in place of 30 the year before. I had done eight of them. I wasn't self employed then. I had to work extra to accrue lieu time to make this possible. The Railway was stretched. There wasn't as much free time then as now.

Is it still necessary for the Railway to be turning away business, for example in the four days leading up to Good Friday when schools are on holiday? In 2003, these four days fell in mid April, they were sunny, there were working members on site and some similar railways were operating.

It is not yet proven, whether a commuter service is practical or justified. In the meantime, it is right that the Railway should exploit the tourist / heritage business - preferably to the full.

4 wheel "railbus" No 79964 at Oxenhope in February 1991. The original declared aim of the Society was to provide such a service every day.   *(Martin Bairstow)*

The Grassington Branch

A "Crab" 2 - 6 - 0 has arrived at Grassington with a ten coach Ramblers Excursion on a rather murky 16 November 1958. The porter is collecting outward halves from passengers as they leave the platform. Even at a station closed for 28 years, the ritual has to be maintained.

(J C W Halliday)

Authorised in 1897 as the Yorkshire Dales Railway, the 8¾ mile branch ran from Embsay Junction to Grassington & Threshfield. Opened on 29 July 1902, the passenger service was an early casualty but most of the line is still in use for quarry traffic.

The branch was a scaled down version of earlier, more ambitious schemes to serve Upper Wharfedale.

The Skipton & Kettlewell Railway
This abortive enterprise obtained Parliamentary sanction, by an Act of 1880, to build a 9¼ mile line between Gargrave, west of Skipton, and Threshfield. The Act referred to the possibility of extending to Kettlewell, another five miles, upon further application.

An Act of Parliament was no guarantee that a railway would be built. It was an enabling measure, granted when both Houses had been persuaded that the public benefit would outweigh any detriment. It was then up to the promoters to raise capital, execute works and, ultimately run the line within the powers conferred.

Instead of building their authorised line, the Skipton & Kettlewell people plunged straight into a Bill for extension, not just to Kettlewell, but to Aysgarth on the NER Wensleydale Line. They were unsuccessful. One of their witnesses was Christopher Other of Coverham Abbey, three miles from Leyburn on the NER. Under cross examination, he insisted that he would collect coal by cart from the nearest station on the new route, 12 miles away rather than from Leyburn, because Barnsley coal was better than that mined in Durham and would "please the females in his house."

Undeterred, the promoters went ahead in the 1882 session with a measure seeking powers to go as far as Darlington. The outcome was the same. They continued to trouble Parliament each year up

to 1884, with variations on their hopeless ambitions. When they came in 1885, it was with a Bill abandoning the 1880 powers, in pursuit of which no construction had taken place.

The Yorkshire Dales Railway
A new generation of promoters came forward in 1895, again with an over ambitious plan to link Skipton with Darlington. A Bill was deposited but then withdrawn as reality began to dawn. The promoters decided on a piecemeal approach, beginning with a modest project for a line as far as Grassington.

The Yorkshire Dales Railway (Skipton & Grassington) Act was passed in August 1897. It permitted a working agreement with the Midland Railway, the details of which had already been negotiated. The local Company was to raise capital and build the line, which would then be operated by the Midland who would take 60% of the income. As with similar arrangements elsewhere, the Midland ended up having to subscribe a proportion of the capital. The "first sod" was turned on 7 June 1900 and the railway opened on 29 July 1902.

Plans for a triangular junction at Embsay had been dropped, during the Parliamentary process, in favour of a connection in Skipton direction only. At first, single line security was by a "one engine in steam" staff issued to trains entering the branch at the new Embsay Junction signal box. The system was inflexible, requiring each train to return to Embsay Junction before another one could be scheduled. In 1904, electric token working was introduced to coincide with the opening of Delaney's Siding, a mile long quarry branch diverging at the entrance to Grassington Station where a signal box was installed.

Stone was the mainstay of the branch. The

siding at Swinden Lime Works was provided from the opening. Since 1969, this expanded facility has been the sole reason for survival of the line.

Upper Wharfedale

Despite the difficulties experienced in financing the modest Grassington branch, it was not until the First World War that proponents of extension finally gave up. Some people see evidence, in the situation of Grassington & Threshfield Station, that the branch was built with extension in mind. Otherwise it might not have terminated so high and so far from the centre of Grassington. There is even the matter of the track layout within the station. The second platform and trailing crossover seem more appropriate to a through station than a branch terminus.

In May 1903, application was made to the Light Railway Commissioners for an order permitting an extension from Grassington to Kettlewell. The promoters were independent of the Yorkshire Dales Railway, which was not in support. Later the same year, some of the same promoters were behind a Bill for a main line extension to Darlington. The Light Railway Order was declined and the main line scheme failed to raise the Parliamentary deposit. Further unsuccessful attempts at a Light Railway were made in 1907 and 1908. The last Bill for a main line extension was deposited in 1912.

The Branch in Operation

The working agreement between the Yorkshire Dales and Midland Companies lasted until the "Grouping" of 1923 when both were absorbed into the LMS. The local Company, which had paid dividends, was in negotiation to sell out to the Midland, regardless of the "Grouping"

The branch passenger service comprised up to seven trains each way, two on Sundays. There must have been some Bradford wool merchants, or other commuters living in Grassington to justify the introduction of a through train in July 1910. In anticipation of this, a facing point lock was installed on the trailing crossover at Embsay Junction so that passenger trains could negotiate it in the facing direction. The 7.45am from Grassington left with portions for both Skipton and Bradford. It came to a stand just beyond Embsay Junction, where the rear coaches were detached. As the front portion continued towards Skipton, a light engine from Ilkley coupled onto the Bradford coaches. The signalman then pulled No 13 cross over followed by No14 ground signal and the train set off for Addingham and Ilkley. Here, more carriages were added for the run to Bradford, reached about 9am. The through working lasted, with minor changes until 1930 but there was never a corresponding through train the other way.

From July 1910, a coach was slipped at Skipton off the 5.10 pm Bradford - Morecambe "Residential". This was attached to the 5.55 pm Skipton - Grassington, giving a 6.23 arrival. Slip coaches were discontinued on the Midland Railway in 1917.

From 1923, the "Residential" stopped at Skipton restoring a connecting service for Grassington. At this time, morning Grassington - Bradford

The driver of 75042 grabs the single line token from signalman Bill Leathley at Embsay Junction, about 1965. Opened with the Grassington Branch in July 1902, the signal box closed on 6 July 1969. For many years it had been open for one shift only. In 1961, the hours were 9.45am to 4.55pm Mondays to Fridays, closing two hours earlier on Saturdays. At other times, the block was normally switched through from Skipton Station North Junction to Ilkley.
(John Robinson/ F W Smith collection)

Standard class 4 No 75011 approaching Swinden Lime Works with the Grassington branch goods on 29 July 1966. Since 1969, the quarry has been the sole reason for survival of the truncated branch line.

(M Mitchell)

commuters had an interesting choice of trains. The through coaches left at 7.33. By then, they had stops at Embsay, Bolton Abbey and Addingham, reaching Ilkley at 8.21. There they stood until 8.30 when they departed for Bradford Forster Square, arrive 9.03 with stops at Ben Rhydding, Burley and Shipley. An athletic passenger could alight at Ilkley, dash under the subway and catch the 8.24 to arrive Bradford at 8.52 with stops only at Menston and Guiseley. An even faster overall journey could be achieved by the 8.03 from Grassington, changing at Skipton on to the "Residential" which arrived in Forster Square at 9.15.

Closure to Passengers

After only 28 years operation, the branch found itself no longer indispensable for passengers. By 1930, the motor bus had demonstrated its reliability and the road network had been improved sufficient to accommodate it. A lot of bus traffic was quite separate from that of the Railway, which on many routes, could offer greater speed, comfort and capacity. These qualities counted for little on some branch lines, where the bus could offer a more frequent service, direct to villages, which the Railway served only in name.

The station at Grassington & Threshfield was closer to the latter village, not very convenient for Grassington itself. The passenger service fell victim in September 1930 to the round of closures, which were prompted by the Railway Companies investing in bus operators. The LMS local timetable for Summer 1936 has two pages devoted to Grassington. It shows the full "omnibus" service from Skipton Town Hall to Grassington, irregular but generally at least once per hour. Then it shows through train / bus connections from Leeds and Bradford, for which purpose about half the Grassington buses are extended to and from Skipton Station. Through fares, including season tickets are advertised from Bradford to Rylstone and Grassington.

Excursion trains continued, many of them aimed at bringing ramblers on day outings to Grassington at Bank Holiday periods. This activity was suspended during the Second World War but resumed at Easter 1949, when minor repairs were made to the platform at Grassington. Besides this occasional activity, the branch remained fully operational for general goods as well as stone traffic. Inward traffic included coal, both for the quarries and for the three coal merchants based in Grassington Station Yard. There was a modest trade in coal and cattle feed at Rylstone. Most parcels were handled by road lorry from Skipton but odd items were carried on the twice daily branch goods. Very occasionally, passengers would be authorised to travel in the guard's van.

Grassington employed two goods porters and two porter signalmen under a Station Master, responsible also for Rylstone, which itself retained two porter signalmen. Writing in the *YDR News* for Winter 2002/3, Jim Winkley recalls relieving at Rylstone as a holiday job, when a student. He found the job "delightful and undemanding", opening the level crossing for the twice daily pick up goods and serving farmers who came to pick up animal feed from the store in the goods yard.

There were about 20 permanent way staff on the branch payroll, also responsible to the Grassington Station Master. The last incumbent, Mr Len Huff, served from 1948 until final closure to general goods in 1969. A member of the Fell Rescue Society, it was he who arranged transfer of the signal box into the goods yard to serve as the Society's headquarters after "one engine in steam" working was re-imposed in 1962. Mr Huff was made redundant in 1969. He continued to rent the Station House, until he discovered, from an estate agent, that BR was selling it. They hadn't bothered informing the sitting tenant. Substantially renovated, it is now a guest house run by Mr Huff's son.

Rylstone and Grassington Stations closed to goods in August 1969. A few weeks previously, Embsay Junction Box had been abolished and the track thence to Skipton singled. The Embsay & Grassington Railway Preservation Society, forerunner of today's Embsay & Bolton Abbey organisation, chartered a last DMU from Skipton to Grassington and back on Wednesday 20 August. Soon after that, demolition began of the mile and a half stretch beyond Swinden Lime Works.

The remainder of the branch did not close as Tilcon took over Swinden Quarry and began to increase output.

During Summer 2002, local authorities commissioned a feasibility study into the possibility of making more use of the branch. Topics for consideration include carrying passengers to Swinden, extending part way towards Grassington and reconnecting the Bolton Abbey line at Embsay Junction.

4F No 44337 passing the remains of Rylstone Station at Whitsuntide 1958 with an excursion from Huddersfield to Grassington via Leeds and Keighley. The loco carries a different reporting number (592) from the leading coach (593) because it has started out from Bradford via Ilkley, left its train at Embsay Junction and picked up the second excursion at Skipton. The handbill (above) shows the standard bank holiday workings to Grassington which required three engines for two trains.

(Peter Sunderland)

Peak hour at Grassington on Easter Monday 1961. In the platform, the 5.55pm to Huddersfield. whose engine will come off at Skipton then travel light to Embsay Junction. On the right, 44041 waits in the goods yard with the 6.30 to Bradford via Ilkley.   *(Peter Sunderland)*

By the Summer of 1968, Grassington was the last steam worked branch line on British Railways. "Standard" 4 - 6 - 0 No 75019 shunting at Swinden Lime Works on 1 June.   *(G W Morrison)*

The Cattle Special

Menston Junction 1949 - 52
By F W Smith

Len Goulding at Menston Junction about 1949. The photo predates the "Cattle Special". Otherwise the photographer might have pulled the signal rather than the camera shutter. Len is perched on the Menston Station distant (No20) which sat below the Menston Junction up home (No 4). Had he really wanted to show off, he could have climbed further up the same post where he would have found another identical pair of arms. The distants were removed when Menston Station box closed on 22 October 1951.

(F W Smith)

I was 17 when I got to know signalman Farrar Fern. I was working for an optical firm in Manningham. On Farrar's late turn Saturday, I would catch the 12.09 from Manningham to Menston, then walk down a path alongside the line to Menston Junction box. Once I entered, Farrar would put his feet up on the locker, pick up his newspaper and leave me to it.

The next train was the four bells express passenger 12.23 SO from Bradford F S to Harrogate, due to pass at 12.44. The three coaches were usually worked by a Starbeck "Hunt". On one occasion, I had pulled off for this train and, as it passed the box, was reaching up to give "train entering section" to Milnerwood Junction. To my horror, the needle on the block instrument was still at "line blocked". I had forgotten to offer it forward and obtain "line clear". I alerted Farrar who immediately offered it, saying "I hope he takes it" which luckily he did. This was followed by "train entering section", by which time it must have already passed Milnerwood's distant at caution.

This was a reminder that the Wharfedale boxes were on "free block". The signals could be pulled freely, without the need for a line clear indication. Only in the 1970s, long after Menston Junction closed, were the starter signals interlocked with the block instruments.

About 1952, I got to know Farrar's mate Len so I then went to the box every Saturday. It was late in November 1952, that Len announced he was going home to Otley on his motorbike to get changed, ready for a dance straight after work. Would I be alright to look after the box for half an hour? As the next train was not due for 45 minutes, I agreed and off he went.

He'd not been gone 10 minutes when I heard one bell "call attention" from Guiseley. I responded and received 1 - 4 "is line clear for unfitted freight?" My mind raced. Luckily, I knew the signalman at Guiseley and he knew that I worked Menston Junction. He told me that it was a cattle special for Otley, one wagon. I could manage this except that Milnerwood Junction box was closed on Saturday afternoons, switched through from Otley to Burley Junction. This meant that the train would have to go via Burley with reversal and run round. It also meant that I would have to advise Burley by telephone. Consternation as the man at Burley was Eddie Binns who would not put up with unqualified youths working a box next to his. I did my best to disguise my voice as Len's. It worked. He said he would have to go out and put lamps in a couple of "dollies" (ground signals). I thought I had got away with it as I offered the train forward and pulled off.

But the driver wanted the Otley line and approached with a series of short pops on his whistle, before coming to a stand at the junction signal. This now meant a walk down the line for me, with hand lamp, to inform the driver that he would have to go via Burley and run round his train. What he thought of a youth giving him the message, I do not know but he accepted it and off he went, much to my relief. It was dark. When Len returned all dressed up, he was glad that I had coped and not dropped him in it.

Four Engines and Three Trains in One Section

I spent a Bank Holiday Monday with Len at Menston Junction. On this day only, a light engine, ex L&Y 2 - 4 - 2T No 50636 was sent from Manningham to act as emergency banker, if required. The trouble was we had nowhere to put it. The only solution was to move it about from one line to another each time a train needed to pass. There was much shouting and waving as most of the moves could not be signalled. When it needed water, the Lanky tank had to go to Burley, where there were columns on the platform ends.

In the late afternoon, a light drizzle began and a return extra from Bolton Abbey stuck after leaving Menston Station. Trains then started to pile up. We had one at the home signal from Burley, another at the home from Milnerwood and the Lanky tank blocking the down line towards Milnerwood. After about 30 minutes, the guard of the failed train arrived to conduct the assisting engine, the Lanky tank to the rear of his train.

40 minutes passed until the fireman of the Lanky tank returned to report that they couldn't shift it and needed further assistance. This was given in the form of the "compound" with nine coaches ex Grassington, which had been standing at our home signal.

Another half hour or so passed until the guard of this train hove into sight, requesting even more assistance. The fireman of the K1 2-6-0, waiting on the line from Milnerwood, was in the box signing the book. He said that we should have let his train in first and they would have shifted them easily. Now he got his chance and was as good as his word. We had four engines and three trains, all hours late, in the section from Menston Junction to Guiseley. The K1 got them moving and they were separated at Guiseley. But we never again had a banking engine to play with at Menston Junction.

A Harrogate to Bradford train approaching Menston Junction about 1936. The signal from Burley was replaced in the 1940s with the co-acting lower arms seen on the previous page. *(F W Smith collection)*

L&Y 2 - 4 - 4T No 50636 passing Menston Junction with the 12.40 Ilkley to Bradford on 26 July 1952. The signal is the higher version of up home No 4, necessary for sighting clear of the road bridge. The distant arm has been removed following closure of Menston Station box. *(F W Smith)*

Embsay in 1958

By F W Smith

Bill Smith joined British Railways as a porter/signalman at Embsay in 1958. His first problem was getting there from his home in Ilkley.

On early turn, I had to open the Station at 7am. I'd been tipped off how to make it there by relief signalman Jack Hutchinson, also of Ilkley, who had been covering the vacancy. He had no personal transport so had used three buses.

Departure from Ilkley was at 5.55am on the Keighley bus as far as Steeton Top, where, within five minutes, a Skipton bus was boarded. This was due to reach Skipton bus station at 6.45, in time for the 6.50 to Embsay, which took eight minutes. All the times I used this method, I was never late.

I was booked off for a 1½ hours lunch break so my early turn didn't finish until 4.30pm. I then had to wait until 4.53 for a train home, but this became 5.14 after dieselisation in January 1959.

In alternate weeks, I was on late turn, which ran from 10am until after departure of the last train. To reach Embsay for 10am, I had to leave Ilkley on the 8.50am Skipton bus, alighting where the Railway crossed the road on the outskirts of Skipton. From there, I walked along the track, through Haw Bank Tunnel and past Embsay Junction to arrive Embsay Station about 9.35. The last train to call at Embsay was the 5.15 Leeds - Skipton, due at 6.20pm. I had already locked up and put out all the lights except one, which I quickly extinguished before boarding the train down to Skipton. This left the one regular alighting passenger, a lady, in total darkness but I never had a complaint.

At Skipton, I stayed on the train, which was shunted onto the down goods road. After a short time, a fresh engine came on the rear and worked the empty stock to Ilkley, which was reached about 7.10pm, the train then forming the 8.40pm to Leeds.

During my seven years at Embsay, I tried other ways of getting there for early turn. One was to get a lift in the brake van of an oil train, which was booked to pass Ilkley at 6.15am. To do this, I needed the help of Ilkley signalman Cecil Chatterton who kept the signals on and stopped the train by his box with a red hand lamp. I then had to ask the driver, both of them if it was double headed, if they would drop me off at Embsay. I don't think they liked it as they first had to draw forward and stop again to let me board the brake van. They slowed right down, but didn't actually stop, to let me off at Embsay.

Some time after dieselisation, an empty DMU was booked to leave Ilkley at 7am for Skipton. With most crews, it would set off about 6.45 dropping me at Embsay just in time for my 7am start. One guard insisted on not leaving Ilkley until 7am and I was late all week, failing to book our two regular passengers on the first train. The Station Master, Mr Turner did not take kindly to this as the station was losing revenue. We only had six regular passengers!

When I arrived at Embsay for the first time on 3 March 1958, I entered into a sort of time capsule. Things were still being done as in Victorian times. The trains were all steam hauled. The lighting on the platforms, in the booking office and signal box was by paraffin lamps. Electricity was unheard of. Even the GPO telephone had a hand generator, which had to be cranked at high speed before each call. The railway circuit telephone was ancient with separate mouth and ear pieces. The signals had oil lamps, which had to be replaced every week. At least this was an improvement from the time when they had to be taken out daily.

The Skipton end of Hawbank Tunnel (219 yards), photographed on the way to work on 5 June 1958.

(F W Smith)

In the booking office, the rack was probably the original. Some of the ticket issues had not seen use for many years. The top tickets in these particular tubes were in the process of partial disintegration.

The toilets were of the chemical variety. Water was obtained from a single tap, outside on a wall in the gents. During winter, this tap was sometimes frozen for weeks on end, despite attempts to thaw it out with paraffin soaked rags. The fire from these raged round the tap until it spat steam like an overloaded boiler.

Embsay Station Signal Box was opened, by the porter - signalman, only when required for shunting. It was normally switched out of circuit, the usual block section being Embsay Junction to Ilkley, between 9.45am and 4.45pm, and Skipton Station North Junction to Ilkley, the rest of the time.

Embsay Quarry was operated by the Skipton Rock Company who despatched large amounts of ballast in special trains and by the pick up goods. Up to three specials were booked to run on Thursdays and Fridays to destinations in the London Midland Region. Empty hopper wagons usually returned on the morning pick up goods from Skipton but could also arrive on special workings. These could turn up at any time, causing the box to be opened at short notice. On occasions, one loaded wagon would turn up in the middle of 20 or so empties. It would have to be shunted out as the Quarry did not want it back. This prolonged shunting was often the cause of heated tempers among the train crew who wanted to be rid of all the wagons in one go and be off back to Skipton.

Apart from signalling, my duties included booking passenger tickets, charging up and forwarding parcels, unloading incoming parcels off passenger trains and entering details on sheets for delivery by road vehicle. I attended the arrival of each passenger train, collected the tickets, sometimes as many as a dozen per shift, and gave the "right away" to the guard.

Each Wednesday, I took out the signal lamps, trimming and refilling them for the following week. The same function was performed with the station oil lamps which, of course, had to be lit and extinguished each day during the winter months, a job which in windy conditions could use a couple of boxes of matches.

Other jobs included emptying the toilets into a hole, previously dug, and washing the station windows. The gardens were well maintained by Station Master Harold Turner, with a spot of weeding by me.

Station Master Turner did his best not to burden BR finances with overtime pay, hence his insistence that I book off for the 1½ hour lunch break. Only if the signal box had to be opened for quarry traffic, would that rule be relaxed. When I was on late turn, the Station Master covered the first three hours from 7am until 10. But he didn't like working the signal box himself. So if he knew in advance that the box would be required to open, economy was tossed

Signalman Cecil Chatterton in charge of Ilkley box about 1953. *(F W Smith)*

aside and he had me in early, on overtime.

Once a year, a wagon of coal for station use arrived on the pick up goods and was placed in the cattle dock siding. The contents were taken, over a period of many weeks, to the coal house in an old MR heavy wooden barrow. The poster boards had to be kept up to date and in good order. Those at the end of the station drive were quite high and could prove difficult on a windy day. I remember getting tangled up with a double size poster, much to the amusement of the watching villagers.

About twice a year, usually in Summer, the District Operating Superintendent would pay a visit with other officials. They would arrive in the "Glass House", the inspection saloon. In LMS days, this was usually hauled by a class 2P 4-4-0, suitably cleaned for the occasion. In later BR days, the engine was normally an Ivatt 2-6-0, not specially cleaned. The impending visit would be known about a week in advance. Everything likely to cause concern would be hidden away. Windows would be cleaned, toilets disinfected and platform edges whitened. The special train would be met by Mr Turner and, after handshakes, the dignitaries would be escorted over the footbridge and into the booking office. After a few pleasantries, the party would be taken on a tour

2-6-2T No 40147 entering Embsay with the 1.05pm Leeds City to Skipton on 3 January 1959, the last day of steam working on the local passenger service.
(F W Smith)

The journey to work was a little easier after dieselisation. A Bradford to Skipton train calls at Embsay during the final weeks of operation in 1965. *(D J Mitchell)*

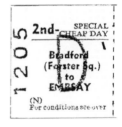

of the waiting room and toilets. They did not linger and, with a few more words and handshakes, they retired to the saloon coach.

During September 1958, new twin car DMUs started to pass through Embsay on driver training, prior to taking over all local passenger workings from Monday 5 January 1959. Apart from the diesels and an improved GPO telephone, nothing changed at Embsay until closure in 1965.

Harold Turner also had responsibility for Bolton Abbey and Addingham Stations. He was provided with a Lambretta motor cycle for travel between his three posts because of the sparse train service. Latterly, Addingham only had one porter, Austin Burdock who finished at 4.30pm, after which the station was unstaffed. In winter, the gas lights were switched on by the porter and off by the guard of an empty DMU which left Skipton for Ilkley at 7pm.

Addingham Signal Box was opened only for the pick up goods which stopped in the up (Ilkley) direction only. Traffic consisted of two or three wagons of coal weekly, dealt with in the back siding.

At one time, a porter - signalman opened the box. When that position was withdrawn, the station master did it. After his removal, the box was worked by a porter - signalman, who travelled from Ilkley by passenger train. To save both time and his bus fare back, the box was not opened on the block bells but operated as a ground frame. This allowed him to return to Ilkley on the goods, rather than have to wait at Addingham for the "train out of section" bell.

The chief operative at Bolton Abbey was Fred Scott who started there in 1931 as a porter. About 1941, the signal box was reduced from two full shifts to opening only for the pick up goods to shunt the yard. The two signalmen's posts were abolished and replaced by a porter - signalman, Fred Scott. As he was also required to attend to all station office work and accounts, the post was upgraded to leading porter - signalman.

In later BR days, Bolton Abbey Signal Box was used on Bank Holidays and Summer Sundays for reversing passenger trains. I got myself passed to work Bolton Abbey box but relief signalmen objected to my taking "their work" on Summer Sundays. So instead, I was rostered for the booking office and Fred Scott for the box. The relief men couldn't object to the permanent leading porter - signalman but we simply swapped functions as Fred preferred the booking office and I the box.

I cycled from Ilkley to open up at 10.10am, but brought my bike back on the last passenger train at 7.30pm, Fred Scott kindly seeing to the closure of the signal box. DMUs used No 14 crossover to reach the up line. There was no disc signal so a duster waived from the box had to suffice. The DMU had to pass the down starter (No 3) so "line clear" had to be obtained from Skipton Station North Junction. No train actually went from Bolton Abbey to Skipton

on a Sunday so the block indicator was left at "train on line" all day until the last DMU had crossed over.

Bolton Abbey signal box would sometimes remain closed for weeks at a time during Winter as very little goods traffic remained. It was open for the last time on 11 October 1964 for loading scrap rails from the sidings, the goods yard having closed the previous April.

Fred Scott was made redundant when Bolton Abbey Station closed. He secured further employment there when the main building was used as an administrative centre for a new waterworks scheme. The occupation lasted two years during which internal alterations were carried out, not least electric lighting.

A bit of overtime could be earned cleaning out the Camping Coach. CC 133, a Great Eastern product of 1912, was converted in 1952 and served at Bolton Abbey until 1964. *(F W Smith)*

2nd- SPECIAL CHEAP DAY
0770
Embsay
to
LEEDS (CITY)
(N)   Fare 4/4
For conditions see over

Fairburn tank No 42093 on a Bradford to Skipton train deposits a handful of travellers at Bolton Abbey in Spring 1958. A relief porter collects the tickets. The garden roller, outside the gents, is for use on the platform surface of stone chippings.
(Peter Sunderland)

(opposite page) A Derby built DMU leaves Bolton Abbey for Leeds on Sunday 19 June 1960. Signalman F W Smith watches for the tail lamp to pass.
(Peter Sunderland)

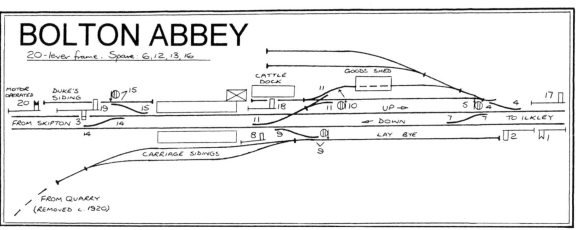

BOLTON ABBEY

20-lever frame. Spare: 6,12,13,16

MOTOR OPERATED
20 M

DUKE'S SIDING

19 — 7 15

15

FROM SKIPTON 3

14

14

CATTLE DOCK

18

8 9

CARRIAGE SIDINGS

GOODS SHED

11

11 10

UP →

← DOWN

9
9

LAY BYE

5 4

7 7

2 1

4

17

TO ILKLEY

FROM QUARRY
(REMOVED c. 1920)

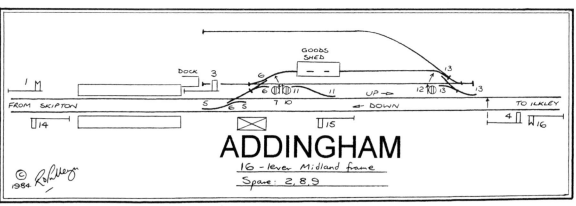

1 M

FROM SKIPTON

14

DOCK

3

5

6 5

6

6 11

7 10

GOODS SHED

11

UP →

← DOWN

15

13

12 13

13

4

TO ILKLEY

16

ADDINGHAM

16 - lever Midland frame

Spare: 2,8,9

© 1984 Rob Mercer

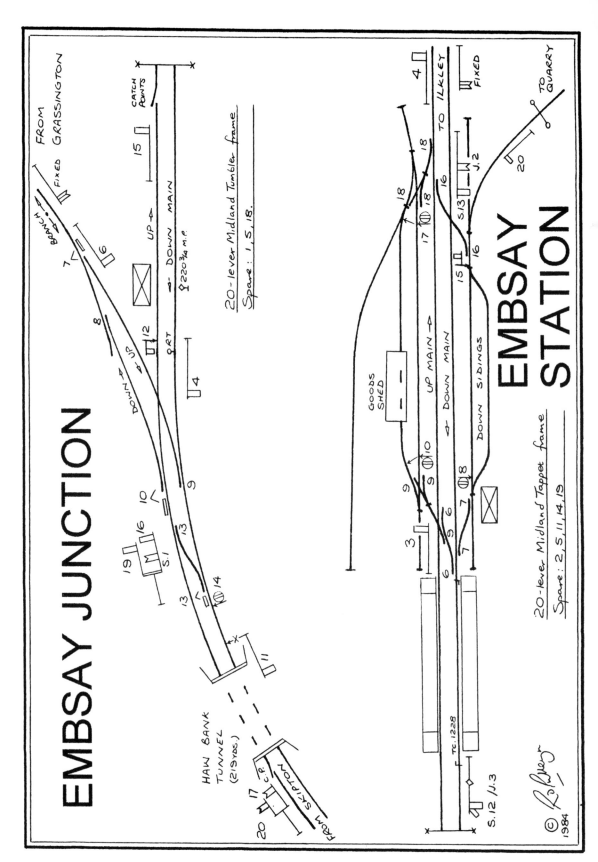

EMBSAY JUNCTION

FROM GRASSINGTON

FIXED

CATCH POINTS

15

UP →

DOWN MAIN →

220¾ M.P.

20-lever Midland Tumbler frame

Spare: 1, 5, 18.

BRANCH

7

6

8

12

RT

4

UP

DOWN

9

16 10

S.1

19

13

13

14

11

HAW BANK TUNNEL (219 YDS.)

C.P.

FROM SKIPTON

17

20

EMBSAY STATION

4

TO ILKLEY

FIXED

18

18

17

18

16

S.13

J.2

16

20

TO QUARRY

15

15

16

GOODS SHED

UP MAIN →

← DOWN MAIN

DOWN SIDINGS

3

9

9

10

9

6

6

7

8

7

7

6

T.C. 1228

S.12 / J.3

20-lever Midland Tappet frame

Spare: 2, 5, 11, 14, 19

© 1984

96

"SPAD"s at Burley, 1976

By F W Smith

Nowadays, signals passed at danger have become national news as the media tries to portray the railways as unsafe. The majority of the ever declining number of "Spads" are without incident. In former times they didn't all get reported.

The 15.30 Ilkley to Bradford DMU was in section between Burley and Guiseley. Approaching from Ilkley was the 15.40 empty DMU to Guiseley, which turned back there to return to Ilkley laden with school children. The empty train was regularly held at Burley waiting the 15.30 to clear Guiseley. On this day, I saw it approaching my home signal at speed. I pulled the detonator placer and grabbed a red flag. The driver seemed to be reading a newspaper but the exploding detonators wakened him and he stopped about ¼ mile towards Menston. After a few minutes, he reversed back to the signal box asking if I was going to say anything about it. Not this time, I replied. The driver was an Ilkley man, noted for passing signals at danger, who never seemed worried about it.

Two days later, the same thing happened with a Bradford driver who was most upset, saying that this was the first time he'd passed a signal at danger. After a word with the guard, we agreed not to report it.

Just as bad, is passing a signal at clear and then reversing back into the section. In the evening peak, a train left Burley down platform for Ilkley. I replaced the starter signal to danger, gave train out of section to Guiseley, accepted the following train then settled down again with my book.

A few minutes later, I heard a DMU horn from the station direction and was astonished to see a train in the platform whistling for me to pull the starter. Against all the rules, the driver had reversed back to set down a passenger who had been asleep. The following train was now approaching my home signal, at danger of course, so I had to get rid of the first train. I pulled the starter but asked the Ilkley signalman to put the driver on the phone when he arrived. I gave him a telling off but did not report him.

Stanier 2 - 6 - 4T No 42682 approaching Burley Junction Box with an Ilkley to Bradford train in Summer 1950.   *(F W Smith)*

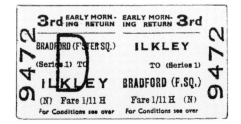

Manningham Engine Shed

By F W Smith

Manningham Shed about 1902 with Midland Railway 0 - 6 - 0T No 1395. The loco was built at Derby in 1878, renumbered 1678 in 1907 and fitted for push - pull working on the Worth Valley branch in 1910. It was withdrawn in 1933.   *(F W Smith collection)*

The first Bradford Shed dated from 1846. Situated close to the Midland Station, it was repairing engines by March 1847. During 1851 to 1853, a second replacement shed was built around the same site.

By 1870, increasing traffic meant that space was becoming very restricted and the decision was made to move the motive power depot to Manningham. Opened in 1872, alongside Manningham Station, the new shed was a roundhouse with a 42 ft turntable and large coaling plant. An additional four road straight shed was added in 1887. Built of wood, it had a slated north light pattern roof, an unusual feature for the Midland. It was demolished during the 1930s but the pits remained for engine stabling and storage. Manningham was coded 29 on the Midland, becoming 20E in 1935. Sub sheds were Keighley and Ilkley until 1935 when Keighley came under Skipton.

In 1879, 42 locos were allocated to Manningham. These comprised mainly 2-2-2 and 2-4-0 tender engines with 0-4-4 tanks for passenger work. There were some Kirtley outside frame 0-6-0s for goods plus a batch of new Johnson 0-6-0s, built by Dubs & Co in 1878.

The 1909 allocation comprised:

Kirtley	2-4-0	21,35,37 38
Johnson	2-4-0	151,152,153,154,217,218,219
Class 1P	0-4-4T	1236, 1240, 1256, 1264, 1265,
		1279, 1280, 1286 to 1301, 1301,
		1351 to 1360
Class 3F	0-6-0	3022 to 3033, 3428, 3435 3800
Class 2F	0-6-0	2309, 2488, 2489, 2491, 2501, 2682
Class 1F	0-6-0T	1640, 1679, 1821 to 1824

By 1920, the allocation had risen to 68, comprising seven 2-4-0s, 30 Johnson 0-4-4Ts, eleven 0-6-0Ts, seven Kirtley and 13 Johnson 0-6-0s. There was also a solitary North Eastern Railway 4-4-0, necessary to work the 7.12 am to Harrogate. A North Eastern driver and fireman were employed at Manningham. They worked to Harrogate, then on to York and then back, reaching Bradford Forster Square at 12.24pm. After that, they returned to Manningham, where both men and machine booked off.

Three new class 2P 0-4-4Ts arrived at Manningham in 1932, replacing some of the elderly ex Midland class 1Ps. Numbered 6402/3/4, they were joined by 6400 in 1936 and 6401 in 1939. Early in 1946, they were renumbered 1900 to 1904. First to be transferred away, in May 1946, was No 1901, replaced by Stanier 2-6-2T No 74. Next to go, in December, were 1902 and 1903, replaced by ex Caledonian 0-4-4 Ts Nos 15130 and 15192. These were joined in March 1947 by 15169 and 15227 replacing 1900 and 1904. The Caledonian tanks were not liked by the Manningham and Ilkley men and were all dispatched back to Scotland by August 1948.

Another class of engine not to fare well at Manningham was the 4 - 4 - 2 "Tilbury " tank, three examples of which arrived in 1938. Nos 2118, 2119, and 2140 did not like the banks on the Ilkley line and were transferred away during 1941.

Around 1928, ex Lancashire & Yorkshire 2-4-2 radial tanks began to arrive at Manningham, where examples remained until dieselisation of Local passenger trains in 1959.

On 11 March 1947, class 3F No 3783 succeeded

in blocking the whole shed for the day when it dropped into the turntable pit, the driver having assumed, wrongly that the table was in the right position for him. Locos were loaned from Holbeck to maintain the service.

An interesting Manningham duty was the 5.50pm from Bradford to Skipton via Ilkley, "Skipton over the top", according to the ticket barrier staff at Forster Square. It was always a goods engine, which worked back on a freight via Keighley. This was my train home from work in the period 1948 to 1958. During 1948/49, the regular engine was vacuum and steam heat fitted 2F No 3078, known to regular travellers as the "Rocket" because of its antiquated appearance.

Performance was anything but antiquated, especially in the hands of a Manningham driver nicknamed "Basher" who thrashed the engine through the tunnels at Baildon and Esholt, showering sparks off the tunnel walls and into the compartments of any passengers, foolish enough to have left the window down.

After 3078 had been transferred away, 3F 0-6-0s became the regular engines, 43742 and 43770 then there were 4Fs, 44216 and 44400. On Tuesday 20 September 1955, I was astonished to find "Jubilee" class No 45639 "Raleigh" at the head of my two coach train. This big engine working lasted six months, during which I counted 48 different engines drawn from five classes. There were 23 "Black Fives", 10 "Jubilees", seven "Standard" class fives, four LNER B1s and four D49s. A small group of enthusiasts gathered at Ilkley each evening to see what would turn up but they soon vanished after the 4Fs returned to regular use.

Nothing larger than a "Crab" was ever allocated to Manningham. The long term resident was No 42762 with 42770 also there for a time. Larger engines visited, of course. In April 1950, two brand new Ivatt 2-6-0 Moguls were delivered to Manningham. Nos 46452 and 46453 were followed in August by new Ivatt 2-6-2Ts, Nos 41265 and 41266. A further new engine arrived in October the

same year in the shape of Fairburn 2-6-4T No 42052.

At the start of 1957, Manningham was transferred to the North Eastern Region, the code becoming 55F. There were 33 engines allocated at that time:

Class 3	2-6-2T	40074,40112/14/17/39/47/55/78
Class 4P	4-4-0	"Compound" 41063, 41075
Class 2	2-6-2T	41247/65/66/73
Class 4	2-6-4T	42052, 42138/39/41, 42380
Class 5	2-6-0	"Crab" 42762, 42770
Class 3F	0-6-0	43553/86, 43742/84
Class 4F	0-6-0	43944, 44216, 44400
Class 3F	0-6-0T	"Jinty" 47222/55, 47419
Class 2P	2-4-2T	50636, 50795

On 25 May 1957, four more engines came under the care of Manningham with the transfer of Keighley back from being a sub shed of Skipton.

Class 2	2-6-2T	41325, 41326
Class 1F	0-6-0T	41855
Class 3F	0-6-0	43178

From 5 January 1959, Diesel Multiple Units handled most local passenger traffic. There was a delay in providing a fuelling facility at Manningham so, at first they to go for fuel and servicing to Hammerton Street, the former Great Northern shed at Bowling. This involved them taking the GN branch from Shipley via Idle.

By Summer 1965, Manningham's locomotive allocation had dropped to fourteen.

Class 4	2-6-4T	42072/93, 42138/89
Class 4	2-6-0	43014/16/30/51/74
Class 3	2-6-0	77001/12
Diesel	0-6-0	D2044/71, D2161

The depot closed on 29 April 1967, when Bradford Forster Square lost its remaining main line passenger trains. The DMUs had all been transferred away eight weeks earlier.

Ex L & Y 2 - 4 - 2 tanks at Manningham Shed on 2 August 1951. 50842 was withdrawn the following month. 50621 survived another three years and is now in the National Railway Museum at York. Both engines worked regularly from Ilkley Shed. *(F W Smith)*

Conditions of Service

A Midland 0 - 4 - 4T calls at Guiseley with a train for Ilkley about 1908.   *(F W Smith collection)*

Bill Smith's Grandfather, Frank Burgess, spent his entire working life in the footplate grade on the Midland Railway, and latterly the LMS.

In 1908, whilst a driver at Keighley Shed, he was issued with a booklet, setting out the arrangements for holidays with pay. The maximum entitlement, of six days for a passenger driver, represented a full week. Goods drivers, firemen passed for driving and passenger firemen got four days but goods firemen only three.

The holiday was not of right but conditional on each driver and fireman qualifying for it by "close attention to enginemanship, more careful working, prevention of smoke and of waste of steam or oil, keeping their engine fronts and footplates clean and smart, etc"

The booklet then lists ten headings, some of which are broken into sub - headings. These were the points "which are recognised as essential to the working of first class enginemen on this Railway." Each point is allocated a number of marks. The total marks add up to 50. When an engine was examined, on shed or out on the road, the crew were expected to score at least 35 or their holidays were at risk. "Mileage" drivers and firemen (the term "top link" is not used) had to score 40. The biggest mark, of 8, was for wiping down the paint work polishing the brass mountings and keeping bright steel parts vaselined in wet weather.

Not mentioned in this booklet, is the holiday entitlement of electric train drivers, a grade only introduced on the Midland Railway in 1908. They got four days, subject to similar conditions.

On 1 July 1912, improved pay and conditions were introduced for footplate grades. It is difficult to comprehend, almost a century later, just what these sums of money meant to the people subsisting on them. As a rule of thumb, the value of £1 was 100 times what it is today. Wages were not then quoted in pounds. An adult cleaner or labourer got 19 shillings a week. That is just under £50 a year, say £5,000 in today's money. That was for a 60 hour week, with no paid holidays, not even Bank holidays.

At the other extreme, a "first grade mileage" driver earned 49 shillings and sixpence basic. That is about £130 a year, say £13,000 in today's money and he would get more if he drove over 150 miles in a day. He got a weeks holiday but might well have to be over 50 year's of age to have reached the position. Differentials were huge.

Shed staff worked 60 hours a week, either six 10 hour days or five longer days plus a short one. A cleaner received 13 shillings a week at age 16, rising by annual increments until he reached 16s at age 19. He could raise this to 18s by passing the firing exam. At age 21 he got 19s a week or 20s at a "large town" depot outside London. In London he got the basic 19s plus the 3s London allowance, which was paid to everybody, regardless of grade, working between St Pancras and Hendon.

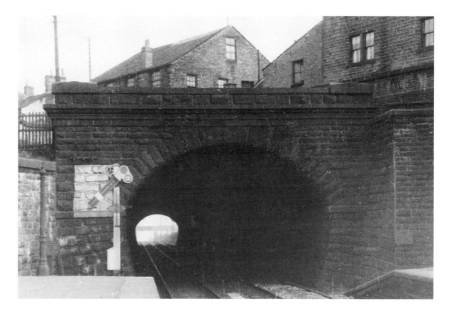

Bingley Tunnel from the platform end. Though badly burned, Frank Burgess was asked to drive his train onto Keighley before getting any emergency treatment.
(D Ibbotson)

The adult rate did not distinguish between cleaners and passed cleaners, those who had passed the firing exam. But a passed cleaner could be sent out as a fireman, in which case he would receive fireman's pay for that day.

Firemen's wages were calculated by the day. This was necessary as a man might only be firing for odd days. For a six day week, the full time rate began at 24s a week in the first year, 27s in the second, 28s 6d thereafter, rising to 30s on becoming a passed fireman, that is on passing the driving exam. A passed fireman would get driver's pay on days when he was sent out as a driver.

The driver's rate was also calculated by the day. The full time rate began at 36s in the first year, 42s in the second and 45s thereafter. If a driver was employed only to do shunting, he only got 36s a week. He could get the appropriate enhanced rate on any day when he drove three miles on the main line with vehicles attached, but not light engine.

The standard day for drivers and firemen was 10 hours. If they went over that, they were paid extra at time and a quarter. If the timetable required, or allowed them to work less than 10 hours, they were paid for the full day. Each day stood on its own. There was a scale setting out the time allowed for preparing and disposing engines, according to type and whether coal was required and, if so, the type of coaling stage in use.

Sunday work was paid at time and a quarter or time and a half, according to the type of traffic worked. Sunday work of any length was subject to a minimum payment equal to that of a standard ten hour weekday. Christmas Day and Good Friday counted as Sundays. Other Bank Holidays were treated as normal days.

The highest rate of pay went to the "first grade mileage" drivers who earned 49s 6d for a six day week, driving express passenger or fitted goods trains. Their ten hour day was deemed to have been reached when they had covered 150 miles. Additional mileage qualified as overtime. The corresponding firemen were also on "mileage".

If the "mileage" men were the elite, the drivers of electric trains were the poor relations. They started at 32s in the first year, just ahead of a passed fireman. They had to wait until the fourth year to

MIDLAND RAILWAY.

Locomotive Department.

NAME *Frank Burgess*

GRADE *Driver*

STATION *Keighley*

Is entitled to an Annual Holiday, with pay, in accordance with the scale given below, providing that the conditions set forth in this book are maintained each year :—

SCALE.

	Days.
Regular Passenger Drivers	6
Goods Drivers	4
Passed Firemen	4
Regular Passenger Firemen	4
Goods Firemen	3

R.M. Deeley

―――――――――――――――――
Locomotive Superintendent.

DERBY, *Sept. 1st* 190 8

reach 36s, the rate for a shunter or first year steam driver. There was no further enhancement. There were only a handful of these men on the Midland Railway, based at Lancaster for the Morecambe and Heysham service.

Allowances were given for lodging turns. These depended whether Company lodging houses were available or whether private accommodation was used. Payments were greater for London than elsewhere. Engine men were expected to take their own food on lodging turns. They were given an extra 6d for food, if sent on a lodging turn without prior notice. Conversely, they were allowed 6d "as compensation for deterioration of food" if they worked an out and back turn when they had been told to be prepared to lodge.

The regime was strict. Breaches of discipline could lead to "fines" being deducted from wages. These were paid into a fund, which began with an annual £1,000 contribution from the Company. The fund was used to make discretionary awards for merit, staff suggestions and in cases of hardship arising from death in service or retirement due to poor health.

There was no guarantee of employment, merely a promise to find work whenever possible. In practice, engine men would have been pretty secure, especially those doing passenger work, for which timetables remained unchanged for years on end.

Born in 1869, Frank Burgess had started at Manningham. He moved to Keighley in the early 1900s, whether as a fireman or driver we don't know. Maybe the move was to secure a job as a driver, which he had clearly achieved by 1908. He drove passenger trains to Leeds, Bradford, Skipton, Oxenhope and probably Ilkley. He shunted Keighley Goods Yard, then a 24 hour operation, with only a hand brake, no steam brake. He suffered a serious injury from a blow back in Bingley Tunnel. He still drove the train on to Keighley, but then had several months off work.

Frank Burgess never got to be a "mileage man". He may never have tried. Instead, about 1914, he moved to Ilkley Shed, where he worked until his retirement in 1934. He then drew his LMS pension until his death at the age of 90 in 1960.

September 1934. Driver Burgess has brought his regular engine, Stanier 0-4-4T No 6402, into platform one at Ilkley for the last time. All that now remains of his driving career is to run round and take it to the Shed. He was destined to enjoy more than 25 years retirement. He outlived the engine by a few months.
(F W Smith collection)

Midland Railway class 2P 4-4-0 No 413 approaching Keighley with an express for Leeds. At this time, Frank Burgess would have been driving more humble tank engines, based at Manningham, Keighley or Ilkley.
(Peter Sunderland collection)

The Embsay & Bolton Abbey Steam Railway

"Monckton No 1 leaving Bolton Abbey for Embsay on 4 October 2003. The loco is a 0 - 6 - 0ST, built by Hunslet in 1953 for Monckton Colliery, near Barnsley. *(Martin Bairstow)*

The short stub between Embsay Junction and Station had remained open, or at least available, for quarry traffic until 19 October 1968. At the time, it looked as though the Grassington line would also close soon. The Embsay & Grassington Railway Preservation Society was formed with the initial aim of establishing a base at Embsay. From there, they hoped to acquire and operate the Grassington Branch.

It soon became clear that traffic out of Swinden Quarry would continue, after closure of the branch to general goods. The infant Society chartered a last DMU to Grassington on 9 August 1969. It then turned its ambitions towards Bolton Abbey.

The first task was to prevent demolition of the track between Embsay and the Junction. This was achieved but only by means of a sit in and some frantic telephone calls when, on 21 October 1968, contractors started work, oblivious that BR had agreed to negotiate sale to the Society.

It took until 1979 for a limited passenger operation to begin between Embsay Station and a point, which they call Bow Bridge loop, just short of Embsay Junction, where connection to the surviving BR line had been severed. Then they began to lay track eastward and, by 1983, could offer a non landing round trip from Embsay via Bow Bridge and then east to Skibedeen. It didn't take you anywhere

until they reached Holywell Halt in July 1987. At last the "line with only one station" now had a destination but it was only a picnic site without road access.

From 1991, trains could get as far as Stoneacre, another non landing run round loop. By this time, the Railway was in serious negotiation with the owner of the track bed, onward to Bolton Abbey. Then, with a combination of volunteer effort, grants and commercial sponsorship, the line was rebuilt to Bolton Abbey. Here the original station lay in the most advanced state of delapidation. The first act was to set fire to it, as nothing was salvageable. Then they began to build a near replica in time for the reopening train, which arrived from Embsay on 16 November 1987.

The Railway operates on Sundays throughout the year, Saturdays from April to October and virtually every day from mid July to the end of August. There are some further midweek operating days which require a detailed look at the timetable. Whilst other preserved railways hold "Thomas the Tank Engine " events to bolster trade on off peak dates, this line does it over the Easter, Spring and August Bank Holiday weekends.

The basic timetable offers five trains each way at 90 minute intervals. Usually, Embsay bound trains go through to Bow Bridge loop, where the engine runs round before returning to the station. Extra trains can be accommodated if Stoneacre Signal Box is switched in.

Most trains comprise ex BR mark 1 open or corridor coaches hauled by industrial steam locos. The nearest to an ex BR engine is 0 - 6 - 0 saddle tank No 68005 which is similar to class J94 but not one which passed through BR hands. On the diesel side, there is class 04 No D2203 and class 14 No D9513 amongst a number of industrials. A three car class 107 DMU operates the timetable on some off peak days.

Bolton Abbey marked the culmination of 29 years effort. At last, the Railway had a destination. A lot of consolidation is still required, not least the provision of under cover accommodation for the rolling stock.

There remains the question whether the Railway will ever run to Skipton. The track at Bow Bridge ends only a few yards from the truncated Grassington Branch. As yet, there is no precedent for a preserved operator to share tracks, which are still part of the national network. It is only a low speed quarry branch with an independent platform at Skipton. Would Railtrack, or its successor, consider access to Skipton at an affordable price and with safety regulations appropriate to a low speed operation, which might be DMU only. Railtrack has donated redundant equipment to the preserved line. Could it demonstrate a similar public spirit by considering such a local scheme on its merit?

The present Embsay & Bolton Abbey operation is a success but almost all the traffic arrives by car at one terminus or the other. They take a novelty ride on the train as part of a car borne day out which may well involve driving further into the Dales. If it could start from Skipton, the Railway would enter the more valuable business of providing car free access to this corner of the Dales

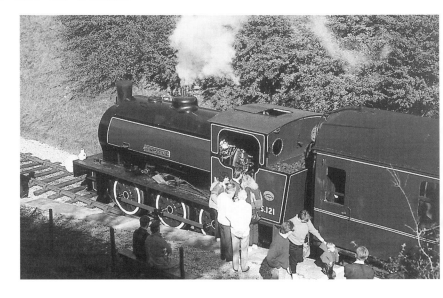

"Primrose No 2" at Holywell Halt, looking cleaner than it could ever have hoped in its previous life at Primrose Hill Colliery, where it featured in *The Leeds, Castleford & Pontefract Junction Railway.*
(Martin Bairstow)

Holywell Halt on 7 October 1990. Now a little used request stop, the Halt was an important stage in bringing the Railway back to Bolton Abbey. *(Martin Bairstow)*

How It All Began

Apperley Bridge, looking towards Leeds on 12 September 1964 from the top of the, by then, open staircase. 42 steps led up from the platforms but there was a goods lift. The figures just visible are leading porter Melvin Marsh and his 12 year old assistant.
(Geoffrey Lewthwaite)

I never intended the book to become auto-biographical. What follows is offered as an insight into the operation of the pre Beeching Railway, which I was privileged to experience at first hand.

By the Summer of 1963, I was in my last term at Calverley C of E Primary School, soon to move on to Bradford Grammar School. My eleventh birthday fell on 1 September that year. Since about February, I had been making the odd train journey on my own, usually between Apperley Bridge and Leeds.

My Father taught at Woodhouse Grove, adjacent to the Railway. Saturday 29 June was one of those days in the School calendar when rail traffic was boosted by visiting parents, some of whom took their offsprings on trips out, such as to Leeds. At about 1.45pm, my Father dropped me off at the station to observe the trains whilst he went to umpire his school cricket match.

Normally, on a Saturday afternoon, the station would be in the sole charge of a leading porter, that is one passed out on selling tickets. On this occasion, the incumbent was a booking clerk, Kevin Swift. He locked his office and came down to the platforms to attend each stopping train, collecting tickets, shutting doors and, when necessary accepting parcels.

The 3.03pm DMU arrived with a sack of sand consigned to Apperley Bridge. Kevin went for a cart. He then summoned me to give a hand. We went across the barrow crossing and up the goods lift to the office, but my task wasn't over. I was handed a clipboard to which were attached lists of parcels awaiting the attention of the delivery van on Monday morning. I was given a pen and invited to write down the details as Kevin read them out. This was called "sheeting the parcels". More consignments arrived by subsequent trains until it was time to go for tea. I walked home, told my mother of my adventure and announced that I was going back, this time by bicycle to save time.

By 9pm, my skills had extended to sorting the collected tickets into numerical order. This apparently futile exercise was abolished during the subsequent 12 months. From every originating station, each type had to be put into numerical order, single, outward half, return half and the corresponding child issues. After the 9.05pm train had gone, Kevin suggested that I should be off home. In those days, it was not considered reckless or unusual for a child to be out alone, especially if he was doing something worthwhile. Kevin knew who I was, where my Father worked and that he knew the Station Master.

For the next 21 months, until Dr Beeching caught up with me, the Station was a very important part of my life. I frequented the booking office and signal box, I helped whitewash the platform edges and maintain the gas lights. I went out with the delivery van, but only once got a ride on a loco - from the platform to the goods yard and back on a 4F.

There was nothing unique in what I was allowed to do. People older than me fired engines on the main line, unofficially. With 40 stopping trains a day and especially with the parcels traffic, Apperley Bridge was busier than a lot of stations. Despite this, the staff were not over worked and, sometimes, the sole person on duty would disappear to the pub between trains. Leading Porter Melvin Marsh, with whom I spent a lot of time, never did that. He did, however, sometimes lock the station and go for a bike ride with me on a Saturday evening between trains. He paid me the compliment of saying that late turn on a Saturday would be more of a drag, without my company.

It was a world, which could not continue. Unfortunately, the remedy chosen was to get rid rather than reform it.

Conclusion

Within my lifetime, the Railways of Airedale and Wharfedale have been to the brink of extinction and come back again. We have long passed the point where increasing road traffic took traffic away from the trains.

In the 1960s, it was argued that an "express bus" could replace the Ilkley trains. In the seventies, someone claimed that it would be cheaper to provide each commuter with a taxi than continue running the trains.

Rising car ownership has arguably been the strongest factor in boosting rail passenger numbers. The cars create congestion, especially in Leeds. They provide access to the rail network, particularly at stations such as Steeton & Silsden and Shipley, where the car park needs further expansion. And car ownership is a symbol of prosperity, which itself generates travel.

No longer is the Railway fighting for survival. The question is whether it can grow further. The potential is there. Demand continues to increase. By the end of the 1990s, the prospects seemed extremely good. Since then, so much opportunity has just been thrown away in a cycle of escalating costs as the true horror of the privatisation fiasco has unravelled. It is fragmentation, not privatisation itself, which is the problem. Its not a question of ownership. Its the fact that nobody is in charge. The National Railway system has become an enormous mirror image of the Worth Valley.

One has to admire the tenacity of the West Yorkshire PTE, who continue to develop rail plans, most of which have little prospect of realisation. The PTE has been behind every improvement, which has taken place, this past 30 years. But they have to beg Central Government for resources.

I fear its going to be a long time before I can return to its proper place, the Apperley Bridge totem, which I borrowed in 1965. It could take even longer before I can throw those tea leaves back into the ticket office at Calverley & Rodley. Put another way, those expensive four coach electric trains will keep running three quarters empty from Leeds to Bradford Forster Square because they don't stop where they might pick up more traffic. The logic for closing these particular stations has long been reversed. Unfortunately, the mechanism for doing it hasn't followed the same change of course.

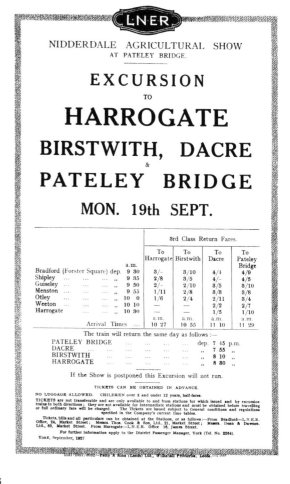

Appendices

Opening of lines

30. 6.1846	Leeds Wellington – Bradford Forster Square
16. 3.1847	Shipley – Keighley
7. 9.1847	Keighley – Skipton
9. 7.1849	Leeds Central – Arthington
1. 2.1865	Arthington – Otley
1. 8.1865	Apperley Junction – Otley – Ilkley
13. 4.1867	Keighley – Oxenhope
16. 5.1888	Ilkley – Bolton Abbey
1.10.1888	Bolton Abbey – Skipton
26. 2.1894	Rawdon Junction – Yeadon (goods only)
29. 7.1902	Embsay Junction – Grassington & Threshfield

Last day of passenger service

21. 9.1930	Skipton – Grassington & Threshfield
30.12.1961	Keighley – Oxenhope
20. 3.1965	Arthington – Burley in Wharfedale
20. 3.1965	Ilkley – Skipton

Closure to all traffic

23. 6.1962	Keighley – Oxenhope
8. 8.1964	Rawdon Junction – Yeadon
3. 7.1965	Arthington – Menston Junction/ Burley Junction
24.10.1965	Ilkley – Embsay
19.10.1968	Embsay – Embsay Junction
9. 8.1969	Swinden Lime Works – Grassington & Threshfield

Passenger Stations

miles				opened	closed	reopened
0	0	0		Leeds City	30. 6.1846	—	
¾	¾	¾		Holbeck	2. 7.1855	5. 7.1958	
		3		Headingley	9. 7.1849	—	
		5¾		Horsforth	9. 7.1849	—	
		9¼		Arthington	9. 7.1849	20. 3.1965	
		10		Pool in Wharfedale	1. 2.1865	20. 3.1965	
1¾	1¾			Armley Canal Road	Sep 1847	20. 3.1965	
3¼	3¼			Kirkstall	Jul 1846	20. 3.1965	
4	4			Kirkstall Forge	1. 7.1860	31. 7.1905	
4¾	4¾			Newlay & Horsforth	Sep 1846	20. 3.1965	
6	6			Calverley & Rodley	Jul 1846	20. 3.1965	
7¾				Apperley Bridge & Rawdon	Jul 1846	20. 3.1965	
9¾				Idle	Sep 1847	Sep 1848	
11			0	Shipley	Jul 1846	—	
			1¾	Baildon	4.12.1876	3. 1.1953	5. 1.1973
			3	Esholt	4.12.1876	26.10.1940	
	10¼		5	Guiseley	1. 8.1865	—	
	11¾		6½	Menston	1.11.1875	—	
	12		6¾	Menston Junction	Mar 1873	Mar 1877	
		12¾	9½	Otley	1. 2.1865	20. 3.1965	
	13¼	15½		Burley in Wharfedale	1. 8.1865	—	
	15½	17¾		Ben Rhydding	1. .1866	—	
	16½	18¾		Ilkley	1. 8.1865	—	
	19¼			Addingham	16. 5.1888	20. 3.1965	
	21¾			Bolton Abbey	16. 5.1888	20. 3.1965	
	25¼			Embsay	1.10.1888	20. 3.1965	
11¾				Frizinghall	1. 2.1875	20. 3.1965	7. 9.1987
12½				Manningham	17. 2.1868	20. 3.1965	
13½				Bradford Forster Square	30. 6.1846	—	
11¾				Saltaire	May 1856	20. 3.1965	9. 4.1984
13¾				Bingley	16. 3.1847	—	
14¼				Crossflatts	17. 5.1982	—	
16¼				Thwaites	1. 6.1892	30. 6.1909	
17			0	Keighley	16. 3.1847	—	
			1¼	Ingrow	13. 4.1867	30.12.1961	29. 6.1968
			2	Damems	Sep 1867	21. 5.1949	29. 6.1968
			2¾	Oakworth	13. 4.1867	30.12.1961	29. 6.1968
			3¾	Haworth	13. 4.1867	30.12.1961	29. 6.1968
			4¾	Oxenhope	13. 4.1867	30.12.1961	29. 6.1968
20				Steeton & Silsden	Dec 1847	20. 3.1965	14. 5.1990
21¾				Kildwick & Crosshills	Sep 1847	20. 3.1965	
23				Cononley	Dec 1847	20. 3.1965	20. 4.1988
26	27¾		0	Skipton	7. 9.1847	—	
			7½	Rylstone	29. 7.1902	21. 9.1930	
			10¾	Grassington & Threshfield	29. 7.1902	21. 9.1930	

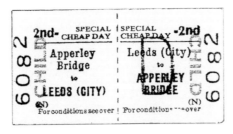
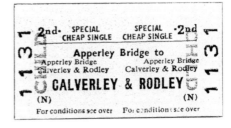

Electric Tramways in Airedale and Wharfedale

"Horsfield" No 203 descending Otley Road, between West Park and Headingley on 30 October 1955. It is working through to Roundhay, allowing Leeds passengers the choice of alighting at City Square or Briggate. A new tramway is planned to follow almost the same route between Lawnswood and Leeds.

(J C W Halliday)

These paragraphs are only a token digression into the complicated subject of West Yorkshire tramways. The topic has a certain topicality, in view of work now planned in Leeds. At one time, I wondered whether the Leeds and Bradford to Ilkley and Skipton lines might become candidates for light rail operation, in the manner of the Tyne & Wear Metro. Instead, they were favoured with main line electrification, whilst light rail is emerging on some of the former tram lines.

Leeds City Tramways

The Leeds system was built to standard gauge. The first lines were laid from Boar Lane, near Leeds New Station, to Headingley and Kirkstall. Opened respectively in September 1871 and April 1872, they were worked by horses and used only to carry passengers. It had been hoped that the Kirkstall line would be used to distribute goods wagons to factories but this never happened. The only goods traffic arose around 1910, when sand and gravel was conveyed from a river wharf in Leeds to a filtration plant at Kirkstall.

Steam locomotives took over the Headingley route in 1883 but were banned in March 1892, following an inspection of the track by Major General Hutchinson for the Board of Trade. The

Tramway Company simply exchanged the steam trams on the Headingley route with the horse cars still running to Kirkstall.

Meanwhile, in North Leeds, the tramway from Sheepscar to Oakwood had opened in November 1891, using electric power, drawn from an overhead wire through a trolley pole, the first such application in this Country.

In 1894, Leeds Corporation took over the tramway system with a view to electrification and expansion. The Kirkstall route was electrified in 1907. It was extended to Hawksworth Road, the Leeds City boundary, in 1906. Then, with the cooperation of neighbouring authorities, it reached Yeadon and Guiseley in 1909, with a short extension to White Cross in 1915.

The authorities in Otley and Ilkley had pressed for extensions to their towns but Leeds doubted the potential and offered a cheaper alternative. From 1915 until 1928, Leeds City Tramways ran a trolley bus system from White Cross to Otley and Burley. The White Cross tramway was mainly single track with passing loops. By the 1930s, the policy of Leeds Corporation was to develop tramways to serve high density population within the City boundary but not to modernise the longer routes outside. The line was cut back to Hawksworth Road in 1934 and to Kirkstall

A steam tram engine, with double deck trailer, waiting in a passing loop by the Skyrack Inn, Otley Road, Headingley. The destination board says Wortley. They ran through to avoid having to run round in Leeds, a principle followed in electric days.

(Martin Bairstow Collection)

They said that trams held up the traffic, but what traffic? "Horsfield" No 253 passing Hyde Park, inbound to Leeds, on the last day of operation, 3 March 1956. Built in 1931 and named after the then General Manager, the 104 "Horsfields" were fully enclosed air braked trams seating 60 passengers.

(R B Parr)

Ex London "Feltham" No 563 passing Leeds Central Station, shortly before closure of the Whingate route in 1956. Previously, this track in Wellington St had been used by services to Kirkstall, Guiseley and Rodley.

(Martin Bairstow Collection)

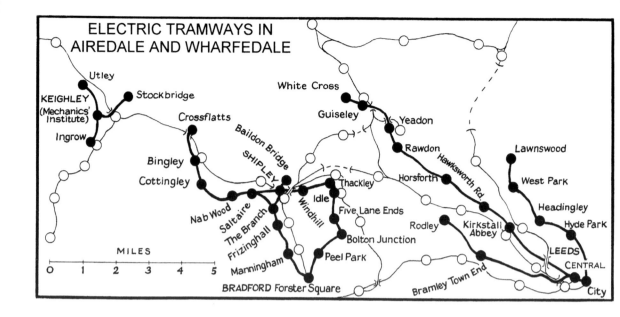

ELECTRIC TRAMWAYS IN AIREDALE AND WHARFEDALE

Abbey in 1949. The only surviving relic is the shed at White Cross, still proclaiming Leeds City Tramways in the stone work.

In 1953, Leeds became one of the last British cities to announce complete tramway abandonment. Kirkstall was an early casualty under this policy, closing on 3 April 1954.

Rodley was served between 1906 and 1938. The branch from Bramley Town End included the descent of Whitecote Hill, at 1 in 8 the steepest gradient on Leeds City Tramways.

Headingley was electrified in 1900. The line was extended to West Park in 1908 and to Lawnswood in 1913. This last section was converted from street to segregated track in 1938. All other lines mentioned were street track throughout. Services were frequent. The 1946 timetable advertises a five minute interval from Leeds as far as West Park, every 10 minutes thence to Lawnswood. The line closed on 3 March 1956, a significant step towards complete tramway abandonment, which was achieved in November 1959.

Bradford City Tramways

The Bradford system was laid to the narrower gauge of 4ft. A horse tramway opened between Bradford and Manningham in 1882, reaching Frizinghall in 1885 and Saltaire in August 1888. Steam power took over, as far as Frizinghall, later in 1888, at which point the Bradford terminus changed from Rawson Square to Forster Square. The gradient up Cheapside would have been too steep for horses. Steam ran through to Saltaire from 1891.

Bradford City Tramways began in 1898, when the Corporation took over and began a programme of electrification and extension. Bradford to Saltaire was electrified in 1902.

The following year, the Mid Yorkshire Tramways opened from the Branch to Baildon Bridge. The Company had wide ambitions, including expansion to Keighley and into Wharfedale. Instead, after only a year, it sold its modest system to Bradford City Tramways who could then operate through from Forster Square both to Baildon Bridge and Nab Wood, 1/2 mile beyond Saltaire. The other legacy from Mid Yorkshire Tramways was completion of the indirect route from Bradford to Saltaire via Thackley and Shipley.

Extension from Nab Wood to Crossflatts took place during 1914 but the two mile gap, needed to meet the Keighley system, was never filled. A mile long extension from Baildon Bridge into Baildon itself was authorised in 1914 but frustrated by the First World War.

After 1930, whilst Leeds was still planning new tramways, Bradford was committed to wholesale conversion to trolley buses. The Saltaire via Thackley route was so treated on 29 March 1930. The Branch to Baildon Bridge closed in January 1936, without trolley bus replacement. On 6 May 1939, trams were withdrawn between Forster Square and Crossflatts, a significant step in the demise of Bradford City Tramways, whose death agonies were drawn out to 1950, only because of the Second World War. History repeated itself in November 1963 when closure of the Crossflatts route broke the back of the Bradford trolley bus system. Saltaire Shed stands as a reminder of both the tram and trolley bus eras.

Keighley Corporation Tramways

Horse trams ran from 1889 until 1904, connecting Ingrow and Utley via the Town Centre. The gauge was 4ft, the same as Bradford. The line was taken over by the Corporation in 1901 and electrified during 1904.

The Mid Yorkshire Tramways Company obtained powers in 1903 for a line between Shipley and Keighley, except that Keighley Corporation insisted on their right to build the last mile into Keighley from the Borough boundary at Stocksbridge.

Opened on 10 February 1905, the Stocksbridge line passed the Railway Station and created a triangular junction at the Mechanics Institute in the town centre. The Mid Yorkshire scheme failed. Under Bradford City Tramways, it reached Crossflatts at the start of the First World War. The link with Keighley was postponed indefinitely. Keighley was left with an isolated three mile system, which closed in 1924 in favour of trolley buses.

These survived only until 1932. They represented Keighley's second venture into the field. The first had included a service from Ingrow to Oxenhope, which lasted for only seven months during 1921. The system involved a small truck running along the overhead power line. It was dragged behind the bus by a cable. When two buses met, the cables were unplugged and exchanged between the two vehicles. There was no passing loop in the overhead.

Effect of Tramways upon the Railways

The trams may have "stolen" a few short distance train passengers but, in the main, their function was separate. No railway service was curtailed due to tramway competition. Most of the tramways succumbed the moment that bus travel became practical. The only hope for the tramways was to become more like railways. Modest steps were taken in Leeds, then everything went wrong.

In 2001, the Government gave the 'go ahead' to PTE plans for a 17 mile tramway system, largely following old routes including between Leeds, Headingley and Lawnswood.

Bradford City Tramways No 93 leaving Forster Square for Baildon Bridge about 1930. Built in 1927, No 93 lasted until 1949 and was similar to No 104, Bradford's only preserved tram, which resides in the Industrial Museum at Eccleshill.
(Martin Bairstow collection)

A double deck horse tram has reached its terminus outside Ingrow Station.
(Martin Bairstow Collection)

1ft 6in gauge "Jack" in steam at the Leeds Industrial Museum at Armley Mills on 23 June 1990.
(Tom Heavyside)

Opened in 1986, the short 2ft gauge Abbey Light Railway operates on Sunday afternoons from Bridge Road , Kirkstall to the Abbey. Ruston diesel No 5 arrives at Bridge Road in September 1990.
(Martin Bairstow)

The 20in gauge Shipley Glen Cable Tramway opened on 18 May 1895 and is still in use. Just under a quarter mile long, it climbs at a maximum 1 in 7 from a lower terminus across the river from Saltaire Station. *(Martin Bairstow)*